Letts

Ultimate Exam Practice

GCSE exam secrets

Steven Croft

English

CONTENTS

To revise any of these topics more thoroughly, see *Letts Revise GCSE English Study Guide.*

(see inside back cover for how to order)

THIS BOOK AND YOUR GCSE EXAMS

Introduction

This book is designed to help you get better results.

▶ Look at the grade A and C candidates' answers and see if you could have done better.

▶ Try the exam practice questions and then look at the answers.

▶ Make sure you understand why the answers given are correct.

▶ When you feel ready, try the GCSE mock exam papers.

If you perform well on the questions in this book you should do well in the examination. Remember that success in examinations is about hard work, not luck.

What examiners look for

▶ There are not normally 'right' or 'wrong' answers in English. The examiner will assess your work on the quality of your ideas and expression.

▶ You should be able to communicate your ideas clearly and effectively.

▶ Your writing should be adapted to suit the purpose and audience you are writing for.

▶ Your writing should be clearly structured and organised in sentences and paragraphs.

▶ Your spelling and punctuation should be accurate and the work presented neatly and clearly.

▶ You should use a wide vocabulary to express your ideas and meaning.

Exam technique

▶ You should spend the first few minutes of the exam reading through the whole question paper.

▶ Read the question you are going to answer through carefully and make sure that you understand all parts of it.

▶ Identify what the question is asking you to do – underlining the key words can help.

▶ Use the mark allocation to guide you on how many points you need to make and how much to write.

▶ Plan your answers; do not write down the first thing that comes into your head. Planning is absolutely necessary in extended answer questions.

▶ Do not plan to have time left over at the end. If you do, use it wisely. Check you have answered all the questions, read longer answers to make sure you have not made silly mistakes or missed things out.

DIFFERENT TYPES OF QUESTIONS

The questions that you will get on the exam papers at the end of the course can take several forms, these are described below.

Essay questions

Often questions that are asked in the GCSE English exam require some kind of essay response. Make sure that you:

▶ Read and understand what the question asks you to do

▶ Plan your answer carefully

▶ Structure your ideas in a logical way writing in sentences and paragraphs

▶ Make sure that your essay has an effective beginning and an effective ending.

Analytical questions

Some questions require close analysis of a text or texts. Very often these types of questions are divided up into several parts. You should:

▶ Read each part of the question carefully before you start to answer

▶ Look at the number of marks each part of the question carries to give you a rough idea of the level of detail required in your answer

▶ Make sure that you are answering precisely what the question asks you

▶ Where appropriate use detailed references to the text(s).

Media questions

Some questions involve looking at some kind of media text or texts. When answering this kind of question you might need to think about:

▶ The language content of the text(s)

▶ The layout of the text(s) including such things as headlines, page design etc.

▶ The use of illustrations and photographs.

WHAT MAKES AN A/A*, B OR C GRADE CANDIDATE

Obviously, you want to get the highest grade that you possibly can. The way to do this is to make sure that you have a good understanding of the various ways in which language can be used depending on purpose and audience.

GRADE A* ANSWER

The specification identifies what an A, C and F candidate can do in general terms. Examiners have to interpret these criteria when they fix grade boundaries. Boundaries are not a fixed mark every year and there is not a fixed percentage who achieve a particular grade each year. Boundaries are fixed by looking at candidates' work and comparing the standards with candidates of previous years. If the paper is harder than usual the boundary mark will go down. The A* boundary has no criteria but is fixed initially as the same mark above the A boundary as the B is below it.

GRADE A ANSWER

A grade candidates can use language in a range of contexts and select and use appropriate styles and registers. They vary their sentence structure, vocabulary and expression confidently to suit a range of purposes. They express and develop their ideas clearly and can analyse argument and opinion and the technical aspects of their writing, such as spelling and punctuation are accurate.

GRADE B ANSWER

B grade candidates show a good level of competence in all the above areas and are able to write fluently with a good level of accuracy.

GRADE C ANSWER

C grade candidates can adapt style and register and use a range of sentence structures and varied vocabulary. Spelling is generally accurate and handwriting neat and legible.

If you are likely to get a grade C or D on Higher tier you would be seriously advised to take Foundation tier papers. You will find it easier to get your C on Foundation tier as you will not have to answer the questions targeted at A and B.

HOW TO BOOST YOUR GRADE

Grade booster ····▷ How to turn C into B

▶ Make sure your vocabulary, register and style suit your audience and purpose.

▶ Write fluently and accurately.

▶ Organise your work effectively.

▶ Make your work interesting so you capture your reader's attention.

▶ Use effective descriptive techniques.

▶ Examine and evaluate ideas.

▶ Show detailed appreciation and interpretation of issues in the materials you are presented with.

▶ Evaluate how language is used.

Grade booster ····▷ How to turn B into A/A*

▶ Produce well-organised and compelling work.

▶ Employ a variety of forms appropriate to audience and purpose.

▶ Demonstrate the ability to use a variety of registers.

▶ Show originality of approach and sophisticated treatment of your topic.

▶ Analyse language use effectively.

▶ Engage the interest of the reader.

▶ Use devices such as humour, satire and irony in appropriate ways.

CHAPTER 1

Writing to argue, persuade, advise

To revise this topic more thoroughly, see Chapter 1 in Letts *Revise GCSE English Study Guide*.

 Try this sample GCSE question and then compare your answer with the Grade C and Grade A model answers pages 9 and 10.

Spend about 40 minutes on this.

Write about 300–400 words.

Leave enough time to read through and correct what you have written.

You have been asked to give a talk to your class on **either** the benefits **or** the disadvantages of mobile telephones. The title of your talk is 'Mobile telephones – are they a blessing or a curse to modern society?'

Write what you would say.

Remember that you are trying to persuade your listeners to agree with your views.

(25 marks)

These two answers are at grades C and A. Compare which one your answer is closest to and think how you could have improved it.

GRADE C ANSWER

*Straightforward and direct opening but doesn't indicate whether speaking from **either** benefit **or** disadvantage standpoint.*

Begins to develop argument to support benefits.

A second benefit developed with clear and logical ideas well expressed.

A third idea is developed in a clear and succinct manner.

A fourth idea is developed with some interesting points relating to language use and text messaging. Towards end of paragraph, though, David begins to talk about the disadvantages and therefore begins to lose focus on the specific instructions of the question.

The candidate continues to discuss the disadvantages, thus moving further away from the focus of the question.

The response is fluent, well-structured, uses an appropriate vocabulary and the spelling and punctuation are accurate. The syntax is clear and accurate and the paragraphs develop the ideas in a logical manner.

David

In direct response to this question I would say that mobile phones are a blessing but do have their disadvantages. ✓

Mobile phones allow younger people to keep in touch with their parents when they are out just so that it keeps the parents' mind at rest. ✓ If an emergency occurs then children can phone their parents immediately to inform them so that maybe something can be done about it.

When there has been a serious accident such as on the roads or motorways then the emergency services can be contacted immediately, whereas before the era of mobile phones someone would have to travel to the nearest pay phone. ✓ During this time someone may well have died. In this sense, mobile phones could be considered a lifesaving device.

Mobile phones are not limited to emergency use though. Many people now use them to organise meetings and social gatherings with friends and colleagues. ✓ It could be argued that mobile phones play a very important part in our society as they promote communication and improve our social relations with others.

The development of 'text messaging' in conjunction with the mobile phone also helps develop relationships with others. ✓ It could also be argued that text messaging also improves our English skills. The restriction of 160 characters per message means that the use of abbreviations is essential and makes us think more carefully about the structure of what is being written as we only have a little space to say what we want. However, as with anything else, mobile phones do have their disadvantages. They are considered anti-social when on public transport such as buses and trains when incessant ringing and beeping can become infuriating to passengers.

There are also some possible health risks involved with the mobile phone as radio waves are passed through the brain. However, they are relatively safe with moderate and sensible use.

Overall, I believe that the benefits of mobile phones far outweigh the disadvantages and the mobile phone is a useful and highly effective tool of communication. ✓

15/25

Grade booster ···⟩ move C to B

The question involved writing on either the benefits or the disadvantages of mobile phones. Although this candidate takes the position of persuading the audience of the benefits, he is side-tracked into talking about their disadvantages too. Closer attention to the wording of the question and the greater development of ideas to support the benefits with no reference to their disadvantages would improve the answer. More awareness of purpose and audience could be shown.

Writing to argue, persuade, advise

GRADE A ANSWER

Good opening – there is a sense of addressing an audience here. Note the use of the rhetorical question – a clear sense of engagement with the audience.

There is a note of humour introduced here.

Goes on to develop the idea and uses examples the audience can identify with to illustrate the point.

Moves on to develop a more serious point here.

Another idea developed here.

Concludes with an unexpected twist and a further note of humour and the overall piece is carefully structured, developing from point to point to have maximum impact on the audience. Original in its approach and written with a degree of flair.

Nasreen

Mobile phones – are they a blessing or a curse? You no doubt all have your own opinions on that topic and, as most of you probably possess a mobile phone yourselves, I expect that you would come down on the side of them being a blessing. ✓ However, I feel that, on the contrary, they have become a particularly intrusive feature of modern life. It seems that you can no longer enjoy a meal in a pub or restaurant with friends without having your conversation disturbed by the piercing warble of a mobile phone. You cannot enjoy a relaxing rail journey, simply enjoying looking out of the window at the landscape flashing past without having your peace disturbed by the tinny sound of an electronically generated version of 'Auld Lang Syne' or the theme tune to 'The Thunderbirds'. ✓

The disturbance caused by the ringing tone, however, is only the beginning. The worst thing about the calls is the booming voices of those answering who insist on speaking several decibels beyond the levels used for ordinary face-to-face conversation. This means you then become the unwilling eavesdropper on the man in the pinstriped suit's latest business deal, the young woman's latest exploits at Club Hedonism or the man in the Queen T-shirt's plans for a 'few pints' after Saturday's match.

A more serious hazard, though, ✓ is posed by those who still insist, despite all the warnings, on using their mobile phones whilst driving their cars. This kind of usage can pose a very real danger to both pedestrians and other road users alike and even 'hands-off' sets are dangerous since the distraction caused by the phone conversation means that the driver is not concentrating fully on the driving.

Add to all this the possibility of potential health risks ✓ from exposure to the microwaves emitted by the phones and it seems to me that the mobile phone offers more disadvantages than advantages to us. Worst of all, though, is the fact that my parents contact me wherever I am. You are never safe from the mobile phone. ✓

21/25

Grade booster ⟶ move A to A*
Although this is clearly a high-quality response, no matter how good the work is, it is very often possible to improve it further. Here are some ideas:
- The use of humour is good and is obviously designed to interest the audience and keep their attention, but perhaps the humour is a little overdone.
- More persuasive points could have been developed on the health and safety issues surrounding mobile phones. Remember that the task was primarily to **persuade** rather than to entertain.

QUESTION BANK

Spend about 45 minutes on each question in this section.

Write about 300–400 words.

Leave enough time to read through and correct what you have written.

Each question carries **25 marks**.

1. Write a letter to your MP in which you argue for or against the raising of the school-leaving age to eighteen.

2. Write a letter to your local council in which you argue for or against the introduction of speed cameras on the road through your village.

3. Write a letter to your local newspaper in which you argue for or against the construction of a ring road around your town.

4. Write an article for your local newspaper arguing for or against the proposed building of a big shopping mall two miles outside your town. Give your article an appropriate headline.

5. The head teacher and governing body of your school have announced their intentions to sell off your school playing-fields in order to raise funds for a new science laboratory. Write an article for your school magazine arguing for or against the sale of the playing-fields.

6. Study the following leaflet carefully. It is designed to **persuade** people to visit the Welsh Highland Railway. Think about the different techniques that are employed here to make the leaflet effective as a piece of persuasive writing.

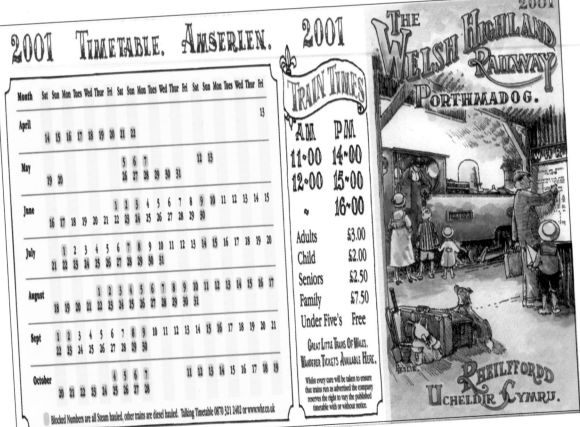

Closed in 1937, assets sold, track lifted, passengers a distant memory – the Welsh Highland Railway was consigned to the scrap heap of history. It had started life in 1872 as the North Wales Narrow Gauge. In 1923 it was extended, and renamed the Welsh Highland Railway. The line had wandered for 22 glorious miles through the remote valleys of Snowdonia – including the famous Pass of Aberglaslyn. It had linked Porthmadog with the isolated villages of Nantmor, Beddgelert, Rhyd ddu and Waunfawr, before terminating, somewhat abruptly, at Dinas just 3 miles short of Caernarfon.

Through the decades the old trackbed had slumbered, but the tunnels and bridges were well made and defiantly withstood the test of time. The railway preservation movement began, flourished and finally focused on the forgotten little line which had blended so perfectly with the idyllic scenery through which it ran. This was to be railway preservation's greatest challenge.

The re-birth of the Welsh Highland has not been easy. However, under the supervision of the FR, work on construction began in 1998, with the first section between Caernarfon and Waunfawr opening last summer. Reconstruction work has now begun at the Porthmadog end. So this year there will be plenty of activity at, and beyond, the terminus at Pen y Mount and work goes on to extend the line a further two miles to Pont Croesor.

Your journey today though is just under a mile. It will include a visit to the sheds where you will be enthralled to see the historic steam and giant diesel locos in their natural environment. You will be encouraged to inspect them at first hand, climb on the footplate and get a real "hands on" feel of a steam locomotive. View the comprehensive display of narrow gauge wagons. Maybe see coach and wagon rebuilding work in progress. Admire the latest exhibit – a beautifully restored Pwllheli horse tram. Understand the working of a narrow gauge railway and the effect it had on the communities it served. The fascination of railways grips the imagination of old and young alike – the unique and unfinished story of the Welsh Highland – 'The Railway that Time Forgot' is without parallel in railway preservation.

And finally, the railway's famous shop boasts the finest collection of railway books and videos available anywhere. If it's concerned with railways you will find it here! Unable to visit in person? – phone Les Blackwell (Tel: 01766 514024), who will provide an unsurpassed postal sales service for just about any book or video. And remember the bookshop is open every day when the trains are running and on Saturday afternoons right throughout the year.

Welsh Highland Railway Ltd., Tremadog Road, Porthmadog, LL49 9DY

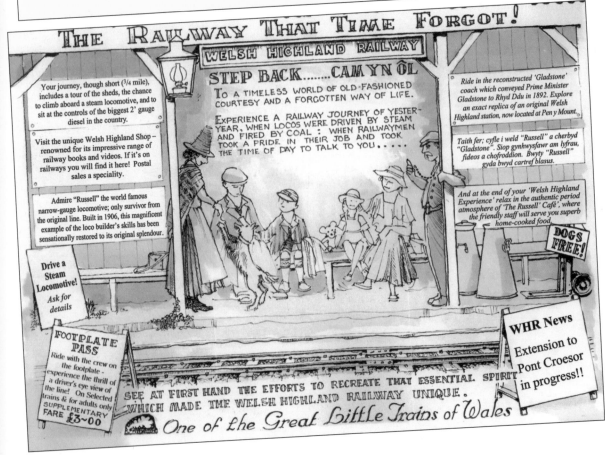

Write a publicity leaflet of your own designed to persuade people to visit an area, town or city or an attraction of your choice. Remember that your main objective is to be as **persuasive** as possible.

7 Write a letter to your head teacher in which you persuade him or her to either abolish or introduce school uniform.

8 Write to a friend to persuade him or her to come on holiday with you and a group of other people from your school or college.

9 Write an advice leaflet for people who have just bought a pet for the first time explaining how to look after the particular pet they have chosen. The pet can be any kind of animal or bird that you wish.

You might write about:

- its feeding requirements
- its housing needs
- its exercise requirements
- any special training/taming/handling required
- any special problems/ailments, etc. to watch out for
- grooming requirements.

10 Write an informative article for a general audience entitled 'Fashions of Today'. When planning your article it might help to think about:

- different kinds of fashion trends (not necessarily only clothing)
- what fashions say about an individual
- whether or not fashion matters.

Writing to argue, persuade, advise

Writing to argue, persuade, advise

EXAMINER'S TIP

General advice
These kinds of questions do not have 'right' or 'wrong' answers and very often they can be approached in many different ways. Here are some general points to bear in mind.
- *Be clear in your mind about the purpose of your writing and the audience you are addressing.*
- *Use an appropriate register and vocabulary.*
- *Write in well-structured sentences and make sure that your spelling and punctuation are accurate.*
- *Make use of devices such as humour, rhetorical questions, etc. if appropriate.*
- *Maintain your reader's interest.*
- *Present your work well.*

❶
- The writing should show a clear idea of the purpose of the task and show a good grasp of the conventions of a formal letter.
- It should be clear whether you are arguing **for** or **against** the raising of the school-leaving age to eighteen.
- It should contain a range of well-developed reasons with clear arguments to support your opinions.
- There should be a clear structure to your argument with points developing from each other in a coherent way.
- A variety of techniques (such as humour, rhetorical question, irony, etc.) add emphasis and give weight to your argument.
- The letter should end in an effective conclusion.

EXAMINER'S TIP

When writing a letter as an answer to a question make sure that you lay the letter out correctly so that it is clear that you are responding to the context the question sets. Never answer a question like this as if it is asking you to write an essay-style response.

❷
- There should be a sense that your audience is your local council and an appropriate level of formality should be used.
- A clear line of argument focusing on the benefits or disadvantages of speed cameras should be developed.
- Specific points should be made and justified – e.g. points supporting the idea of cameras reducing speed and therefore accident rates

or the charge that they are a way of raising money through penalising motorists.
- Your arguments should be logical and clearly structured.
- You should use a variety of techniques to support your points and add impact to them.
- Your answer should end with an effective conclusion.

EXAMINER'S TIP

Make sure you are writing in the appropriate register for this kind of task. Your words will carry more weight if they are firmly put, but make sure your argument is controlled and reasoned.

❸
- There should be a sense that your audience is the readership of your local newspaper and an appropriate level of formality should be used.
- A clear line of argument focusing on the benefits or disadvantages of the construction of the ring road should be developed.
- Specific points should be made and justified – e.g. points supporting the traffic relief that would be brought to the town or the destruction of greenbelt areas, etc.
- Your arguments should be logical and clearly structured.
- You should use a variety of techniques to support your points and add impact to them.
- Your answer should end with an effective conclusion.

EXAMINER'S TIP

Be specific in your comments rather than make broad generalisations. Thinking about environmental issues you might have heard of or that have been in the news could help.

❹
- Your response should capture the style and tone of a newspaper article.
- Your argument should be clearly for or against the proposed building of the shopping mall.
- You should include specific points to support your argument.
- Your article should be effectively structured.
- You should use language to try to convince your reader of the strength of your argument.

EXAMINER'S TIP

Be aware of the kind of style and tone that newspaper articles use and think of a really eye-catching headline.

⑤ • Your style and tone should be appropriate for a school newsletter.
  • Your line of argument should be clear.
  • Specific points should be included to support your ideas, focusing on the playing-field/science laboratory.
  • Your article should convince the reader of your points of view.

EXAMINER'S TIP

Apart from the specific points you make to support your argument, some personal comment from your viewpoint as a student at the school could help to make your article more effective.

⑥ • Your response should be in the form of some kind of leaflet.
  • You should consider aspects such as layout and the use of sub-headings, bullet points, text boxes etc.
  • Your information should be clearly presented.
  • You should use language persuasively.
  • Pay attention to details such as opening times, location, facilities etc.

⑦ • Your answer should be in the form of a letter.
  • It should be clear whether you are arguing in favour or against school uniform.
  • You should use as many ideas as you can to persuade the reader of your point of view.

EXAMINER'S TIP

Adopt an appropriate tone and style for writing to your head teacher.

⑧ • The form your writing is to take is not specified so the choice is yours – it could be a note or an informal letter, for example.
  • You are writing to your friend so you should use the appropriate tone and register.
  • Remember that you are trying to persuade, so your points should be convincing.

EXAMINER'S TIP

Make the holiday sound as attractive as possible and try to anticipate any worries or negative points your friend may feel and reassure him/her that such worries are unnecessary.

⑨ • Your advice should be clear and logically organised.
  • You should write about a range of ideas and aspects of looking after your chosen pet.
  • Use an appropriate tone and vocabulary and avoid being too technical or using words or terms that your reader might not understand (or if specialist terms are necessary then explain them).

EXAMINER'S TIP

Use the bullet points that you are given in the question to give you ideas and help you structure your response.

⑩ • The purpose of the article is to inform, so you need to include specific information here.
  • Use the bullet points to help guide your response.
  • Your writing should be appropriate to the title 'Fashions of Today'.
  • Your personal views on the fashions of today are needed.

EXAMINER'S TIP

'Fashions' here can be interpreted either in a narrow sense as applying to clothes or you can interpret it more broadly if you wish.

CHAPTER 2

Writing to explore, imagine, entertain

To revise this topic more thoroughly, see Chapter 2 in Letts *Revise GCSE English Study Guide*.

 Try this sample GCSE question and then compare your answer with the Grade C and Grade A model answers on pages 17 and 18.

Spend about 45 minutes on this.

Write a story entitled 'A Friend in Need'.

The quality of your writing is more important than its length. As a guide, think about writing between one and two sides of A4 paper.

(25 marks)

These two answers are at grades C and A. Compare which one your answer is closest to and think how you could have improved it.

GRADE C ANSWER

Tony

A Friend In Need

Dave and John were having a kick around on the field behind the quarry. The grass and weeds around the edge were a couple of feet high and the ball kept going into the grass and out of site so it took them ten minutes to find it. ✓ The field that they played on was always full of broken bottles so they had to be careful and make sure they didn't fall, but it was the only large patch of grass where they lived.

They had just started to enjoy themselves when a gang of about twelve young thugs walked past. John recognised them immediately, they walked around looking for trouble anywhere and he knew that they would come over if they saw them. Just as John was about to tell Dave to be quiet and hide ✓ they were spotted. The gang had started to walk over to them. They could not run off now the gang was too close and they surely would be caught and get hurt even worse than they would anyway. Dave and John just stood there froze to the spot. The gang stood around, then one of them walked up to Dave and snatched the ball off of him. Dave wasn't going to argue, he was much smaller than the gang member and they were outnumbered. ✓

The gang just started to play with the ball, they played with it for half an hour until one of them deliberately kicked the ball up and over the fence of the quarry then they just strolled off laughing. John started to search the fence for a way in. Dave tried to stop him telling him that it was only a ball but John wouldn't listen he was determined to get his ball back. He found a small hole in one of the corners and started to unwind the wire until there was a hole large enough for him to fit through. ✓

Stood at the edge of the quarry he could see the ball at the bottom. The quarry was empty because everybody was on strike so he started to climb down. His fingers were still sweaty from when the gang was there so his grip was very poor, he wasn't strong enough to get all the way to the bottom and his legs and arms gave way. He fell down the ridged surface bouncing off large boulders that were sticking out. When he hit the bottom there was a loud crunch and his leg folded up on its self, his clothes were ripped, he was covered in cuts and he had blood running out of his ears.

Dave heard the scramble and went to have a look, when he

Good opening that sets the scene and introduces the characters quickly.

The story develops quickly and there is an element of tension and conflict introduced here which keeps the reader's interest.

Sentence structure needs attention but also some effective description.

SPELLCHECK!

sight
off him
standing
itself

Writing to explore, imagine, entertain

17

saw John lying there at the bottom he thought he was dead. Dave ran as fast as he could to the nearest house and started to bang on the door until someone eventually opened it. It was an old woman with a blue flowery dress on. Dave explained to her as fast as he could and phoned an ambulance and the fire brigade. ✓

Storyline is effective but the ending is rather sudden and abrupt.

They turned up not long after he called them and he showed them where John was. They quickly got to work, the fire brigade put on their mountain rescue gear and absaled to the bottom. They carefully strapped John to a stretcher and put a neck brace on him. Slowly they raised up the side of the quarry until he was at the top and the paramedics took over, put him in the ambulance and let Dave sit with him.

Overall some good description here and the writing is generally accurate, although there are some spelling errors.

It took quite a few months for him to recover and he had lost his memory for his childhood but it gradually came back to him.

When he got out of hospital the council had turned a large derelict plot of land into a playing field with football nets and swings for young children. ✓

16/25

Grade booster ····> move C to B

- The conclusion of the story could have been more developed and effectively structured to avoid the rather sudden ending. Make sure that you think carefully about how to end your story. The ending can make all the difference between a good and a mediocre story.
- Attention should be paid to technical accuracy, particularly spelling and sentence structure.

GRADE A ANSWER

An unusual approach is adopted through the use of diary format. Use of language appropriate to diary form.

Andrew

A Friend in Need

Monday 12 November 2001

This morning I awoke bright and early. Feeling rather refreshed from a good nights sleep. I stayed in sunday evening. For a change. Just me, myself and I. With a video and a take away pizza, curled up on the settee like a fat cat laid infront of a warm fire. ✓ Today has been a funny one. It all started with a phone call which infact woke me up. It was about 7.45am. Strange some one phoning me at that time. Who would want to phone me at that early hour. When I answered, who should be on the other side but my old friend James Wood. Me and James go back along way. I regret it now but I was off hand with him as he had just woken me up, and Im never at my best when I have just woken up. Never the less the day I had planned went off with a bang and I enjoyed my day off work, almost cherishing every moment. ✓

Effective description and relaxed style.

Tuesday 13 November 2001

This morning I arose early feeling like something a dog would have dragged in. I did not feel like I had rested for a week. I felt like I had been up most of the night training for the next Olympic Games. ✓ With that thought in mind, I rolled over and went back to sleep. The rest of the day was spent sleeping or lying down watching my portable television from the comfort of my bedroom. Work called about lunch time and I told them that I was coming down with something.

Use of colloquialisms appropriate to context here.

Wednesday 14 November 2001

Today I feel really rough and washed out so I have phoned the doctor's surgery and asked if a doctor would behable to come out to my house to treat me. The doctor is unable to make it until Friday this week. What if I pop my clogs before he arrives. I think to myself. ✓ Today I have spent it yet again in the comfort of my bed, alone, sick, and untreated. Work called again, and asked that when I return to work I take them a sick note.

Some spelling errors here.

Thursday 15 November 2001

Only another day to go and the doctor will be arriving with some magic pills or poisions to make me live again. No one has called today. I feel a little lonely now and I'm feeling sorry for myself. What I would do now for a friendly chat, with one of my old friends. Laughter is believed to be as good as medicine in some cases. My friends really do make me laugh and always manage to cheer my up when I am down.

An effective ending relating back to title. Overall a lively and entertaining style.

Friday 16 November 2001

The doctor has just been. He has given me a course of antibiaotics and told me to rest until next week. It turns out all I was suffering from was a bad case of Flu. All I could do with now is a friend to call around or phone me up. I wish now that I had'nt been so off with James. It's true what they say. A friend in need is a friend indeed.

21/25

SPELLCHECK!

be able
poisons
cheer me up
antibiotics
hadn't

Grade booster ⋯⟩ move A to A*

- Some of the entries could have been developed a little more. Make sure that you always develop your ideas fully but, on the other hand, don't become too 'wordy'.
- There are a few spelling errors here. An A* answer should be almost error free.

Spend about 45 minutes on each question in this section. Each question carries **25 marks**.

1 Write a story beginning:
'You know I'm right!' said a smug voice from behind me.

2 Write an essay entitled 'The Worst Moment of My Life'.
You may write **either** using an imaginary situation **or** from your own experience.

3 Choose **one** of the following subjects for your writing.

The quality of your writing is more important than its length. As a guide, think about writing between one and two sides.

a) Write about a time when you experienced fear.

b) The Party

c) Continue the following:

'The sun was shining and there was not a cloud in the sky,

but inside I had a sinking feeling…'

d) I thought the day would never end.

e) Write a story which ends with these words:

'…and don't let it happen again.'

4 Write about a time when you have felt anger, jealousy, or excitement and explore the effects of that emotion on you and those around you.

5 Write a story entitled 'The Journey of a Lifetime'.

Your writing can be based on your own experiences or an imaginary situation.

6 Write a talk to give to your class about a book that you have enjoyed and that you would recommend to them. You should focus on the following points in your talk:

- why you chose the book
- what you liked about the plot
- the characters and how the writer presents them
- what you liked about the style in which it was written
- what effect reading the book had on you.

7 Write about a famous figure from history whom you would like to have met, explaining the reason for your choice.

8 Write a short story with the title 'Don't Count Your Chickens'. Your story may be about anything you like but it must suit the title given here.

Writing to explore, imagine, entertain

9 Choose one of the following as the starting point for a piece of writing. The quality of your writing is more important than its length. As a guide, think about writing between one and two sides.

a) One of the gang

b) Too silly for words

c) Write a story involving three people, a boat, a dog and a missing necklace.

d) Use the following as the start to your story:

'When I awoke, everyone had gone and I was left completely alone'

e) Moving house

10 Write a review of a film or television programme that you have seen recently. Your key purpose here is to entertain your reader.

11 Explore the thoughts that went through your mind when **either**:

a) you received some good news, **or**

b) you experienced some kind of crisis.

12 Write an essay entitled 'I wish I could turn the clock back'.

You may write either about an imaginary situation or from your own experience.

Writing to explore, imagine, entertain

EXAMINER'S TIP

General advice
These kinds of questions do not have 'right' or 'wrong' answers and very often they can be approached in many different ways. Here are some general points to bear in mind.

- *Be clear in your mind about the purpose of your writing and the audience you are addressing.*
- *Use an appropriate register and vocabulary.*
- *Write in well-structured sentences and make sure that your spelling and punctuation are accurate.*
- *Make use of devices such as humour, rhetorical questions, etc. if appropriate.*
- *Maintain your reader's interest.*
- *Present your work well.*

① • Your story should begin with the words you are given in the question. These should not be changed in any way.
- Your story should have a carefully planned plot or storyline.
- It should be well told and keep the reader's attention throughout.
- A varied vocabulary should be used and the writing should be technically accurate.
- The ending of your narrative should be carefully thought out so as to round the story off effectively.

EXAMINER'S TIP

It is essential here that you use the exact beginning that you are given and that your story develops from there. Other than that requirement, though, the task is very open ended and you can respond to it in many different ways. Careful and thoughtful planning is very important here so that you know how your story is going to develop and end before you start writing.

② • Your writing should be carefully planned and structured.
- The content of the essay must be appropriate to the title 'The Worst Moment of My Life'.
- Remember that you can base your writing on your own experience or write from your imagination.
- A varied vocabulary should be used and your writing should be technically accurate.
- Your ending should be carefully thought out

and designed to give maximum impact to your story.

③ • Your writing should fit the subject that you have chosen from the selection.
- It should show careful planning and follow an effective structure.
- Your writing should engage the reader's interest and show good use of the imagination.
- A varied vocabulary should be used and the writing should be technically accurate.
- Your writing should have an effective ending.

EXAMINER'S TIP

If you are given a question like this that offers you a number of choices, make sure you think carefully about the option you choose. Making the right choice of title or topic is essential if you are to achieve a successful answer.

④ • The question invites you to write from a personal point of view.
- Your response should explore one of the emotions mentioned – anger, jealousy or excitement.
- Your answer, as well as focusing on an exploration of your chosen emotion, should also focus on its effects on those around you.
- Your writing should be carefully planned and structured.
- It should engage your reader's interest and give a vivid description of the effects of the emotion you have chosen.

EXAMINER'S TIP

Choose something that you have actually experienced to write about. This can often help to make your writing more convincing and effective.

⑤ • Your story should be appropriate for the title – 'The Journey of a Lifetime'.
- It should be carefully planned and structured.
- Your writing can be totally imaginary, based completely on your actual experience or a mixture of both.
- You should use a varied vocabulary and your writing should be technically accurate.
- Your writing should keep the reader's interest throughout and have an effective ending.

6.
- Your writing should be in the form of a talk.
- Choose a book you have something to say about.
- Your writing should show careful planning and follow an effective structure.
- Your writing (talk) should engage the reader's (listener's) interest.
- A varied vocabulary should be used and the writing should be technically accurate.
- Your talk should have an effective ending.

7.
- Careful selection of a figure you have something to say about is important.
- Your writing should be carefully planned and structured.
- A varied vocabulary should be used and the writing should be technically accurate.

8.
- Your story should begin with the words you are given in the question (these should not be changed in any way).
- Your story should have a carefully planned plot or storyline.
- It should be well-told and keep the reader's attention throughout.
- A varied vocabulary should be used and the writing should be technically accurate.
- The ending of your narrative should be carefully thought out so as to round the story off effectively.

EXAMINER'S TIP

It is essential here that you use the exact beginning that you are given and that your story develops from there. Other than those requirements, though, the task is very open ended and you can respond to it in many different ways. Careful and thoughtful planning is very important here so that you know how your story is going to develop and end before you start writing.

9.
- Your writing should fit the title that you have chosen from the selection.
- It should show careful planning and follow an effective structure.
- Your writing should engage the reader's interest and show good use of the imagination.
- A varied vocabulary should be used and the writing should be technically accurate.
- Your writing should have an effective ending.

EXAMINER'S TIP

If you are given a question like this that offers you a number of choices, make sure you think carefully about the option you choose. Making the right choice of title or topic is essential if you are to achieve a successful answer.

10.
- Your writing should be carefully planned and structured.
- The content should be in the form of a review.
- Remember that your writing must be based on a film or television programme you have seen.
- A varied vocabulary should be used and your writing should be technically accurate.
- The review should entertain your reader.

EXAMINER'S TIP

'Entertain' does not necessarily mean that your review must be funny. You may decide to write your review in an amusing way but you could adopt a different approach if you wished.

11.
- Your writing should fit the title that you have chosen from the selection.
- It should show careful planning and follow an effective structure.
- Your writing should engage the reader's interest and show good use of the imagination.
- A varied vocabulary should be used and the writing should be technically accurate.
- Your writing should have an effective ending.

12.
- Your writing should fit the title.
- It should show careful planning and follow an effective structure.
- Your writing should engage the reader's interest and show good use of the imagination.
- A varied vocabulary should be used and the writing should be technically accurate.
- Your writing should have an effective ending.

Writing to explore, imagine, entertain

Writing to analyse, review, comment

To revise this topic more thoroughly, see Chapter 3 in Letts *Revise GCSE English Study Guide.*

 Try this sample GCSE question and then compare your answer with the Grade C and Grade A model answers on pages 26–28.

Read the following extract, which is taken from *A Curlew in the Foreground*, in which the author describes his arrival on the island of North Uist in the Outer Hebrides. When you have finished your reading, answer the questions which follow.

You should spend about 45 minutes on this question.

North Uist is a roughly circular island of about 15 miles diameter and is served by a road which follows the coast. A car ferry operates between Uig in Skye and Lochmaddy. Lochmaddy, the island's port and only town, is in the south-east. My destination was a croft called The Glebe, near the township of Hougharry in the extreme north-west. The map indicated an obvious route leaving Lochmaddy and turning west for 12 miles to the west coast, then turning north. Six miles up the west coast is the township of Bayhead, second in size of the North Uist settlements; and 4 miles north of Bayhead, the turning to The Glebe was on my right. All very simple, and if I lost my way towards the end of my journey, I would only have to ask anyone for The Glebe's owner, a Mr Murdo Macdonald.

The sheer unfamiliarity of the terrain was confusing. No map could give a true impression of this landscape. For one thing, the broad red line indicating the 'A' class trunk road on the map and travelling reasonably directly, was in fact a tortuous little single track which twisted around loch sides and bog hollows and defied all sense of direction. The landscape seen by van headlights was alarming: so much water, sometimes on each side of the road, that I might still be travelling by ferry. Between areas of water were strips of heather and moor grasses shrunken by strong wind and onto everything rain poured down.

Not surprisingly in this inhospitable landscape, there was no settlement once Lochmaddy was passed. It was a world inhabited only by wind and rain. There seemed no alternative but to follow the road wherever it was going, so I drove slowly for what seemed a long way over this island, mile after mile of watery nightmare.

Settlement was reached again at the island's west coast and there was immediate change from uninhabited watery moorland to croftland with many houses. At the roadside now were wire fences, wintry grasses and areas of reeds and rush. I turned north into an even stronger wind, and after a mile or two of confident driving began to be bewildered again. According to the map a couple of minor townships occurred before Bayhead. But there were houses all the way on each side of the road, like one continuous township. Any of the houses on the right might be The Glebe, with a family inside anxiously waiting for me to appear.

Nothing for it but to stop and ask the way of someone. I saw a house near the road and parked on the track leading up to it. Battling with the van door to open it against the wind, I was immediately aware of that smell which was to become so familiar. A compound of seaweed and rain and peat-smoke, acid and invigorating and mixed with the universal hill-farm smell of sheep.

I fumbled with the wire and string which fastened the gate, then clambered over and fought my way up the path to the house. One window showed light dimly behind a heavy curtain. A dog in an outhouse began to bark ferociously. Had the animal been free, my welcome to Uist would have been a thorough mauling. The door of the house was opened slightly and someone called out in Gaelic. A curse for me or a greeting, or a rebuke for the barking dog? I answered in my English and the door opened widely. A mild-faced, silvery-haired old man stood there, shepherd's crook in one hand, the other hand holding the door steady against the wind. You have to step into a house in Uist, the wind won't let you introduce yourself over the doorstep. In the half-lit hallway I shook rain off my coat and apologised for the intrusion. The question, softly and impersonally spoken, was often to be my first greeting from an islander.

'And tell me now, is this the first time you are here?'

The curiosity was detached but sincere, inviting further explanation. I said something about filthy weather and late ferries, then asked please where a Mr Macdonald might be found. I was sorry to seem in a hurry but then you see Mr Macdonald was expecting me.

'Well my name itself is Mr Macdonald.' I might have supplied the 'And I'm not expecting you at all', but the old man smiled in gentle amusement. 'We're all Macdonalds, here.' Of course, the Macdonalds of the islands. I gave more details.

'Ah yes, it's Murdo Iain Macdonald, Glebe, that you're after. A second cousin of mine. A fine man, O aye, a grand fellow.'

The old man in his own good time gave me clear directions. Five miles to Bayhead, and then The Glebe was on my right at the top of a steep hill. The house stood far back from the road and the turning was through white gateposts.

from A Curlew in the Foreground *by Philip Coxon*

1 What impression do you form of the island of North Uist from this extract?
   You must refer to the text to support your comments.   [8]

2 What do you learn about the lifestyle of the inhabitants of this island?
   Use the text to support your ideas.   [8]

3 Analyse the ways in which the author uses language to convey a sense of the
   atmosphere of the island and his own responses to his experiences there.
   You must use details from the text to support your ideas.   [9]

                                                            (Total 25 marks)

These two answers are at grades C and A. Compare which one your answer is closest to and think how you could have improved it.

GRADE C ANSWER

Addresses the question but doesn't enlarge.

Now goes on to expand on view expressed.

Support from text.

Some supporting ideas here.

Good focus on vocabulary.

A further point made here but could be developed more.

Another comment on 'impression' but again could be developed further.

Sound comment and focus on question with textual support.

Not really a 'lifestyle' point.

Valid point but not clear how this quote supports it.

Good focus on language again.

Gemma

1. The impression that we form from the island of North Uist is that it isn't really a very nice place. ✓

First of all the man has been given vague directions for the place he is looking for as we can see in the text '12 miles to the west coast, then turning north. Six miles up to west coast is the town of Bayhead, second in size of the North Uist settlements, and 4 miles north of Bayhead, the turning to the Glebe was on my right.' ✓

As soon as he arrived at The Glebe things weren't going off to a cracking start either: ✓ when he opened the van door the smell 'which was to become so familiar. A compound of seaweed and rain and peat-smoke, acid and invigorating and mixed with the universal hill-farm smell of sheep.' The weather also wasn't exactly as bright as a summer's day was 'a world inhabited by only wind and rain'. The landscape was 'inhospitable', ✓ hilly and rural area.

However, when he stopped and went to a house to ask for a further set of directions he soon changes his mind. The people were all very friendly, very welcoming.

Then he found out that 'we're all Macdonalds here' and that they are all related ✓ 'Ah yes, it's Murdo Iain Macdonald, Glebe, that you're after. A second cousin of mine. A fine man, O aye, a grand fellow.'

It seems that they all are fairly laid back and relaxed about the time, as we can also see in the text. 'Don't worry, he won't be expecting you at any particular time.' ✓   5/8

2. We learn that the lifestyle of the inhabitants on this island is that they have got jobs and they are very hardworking. They live in quite harsh surroundings in a sort of 'watery nightmare'. ✓

The people are also clear and straight forward, they get straight to the point. They also are laid back otherwise the man wouldn't have invited the visitor into the house straight away.

I think that they would be very very traditional ✓ - not up to date e.g. their houses, we notice this in the text 'one window showed light dimly behind a heavy curtain'. And 'In the half-lit hallway I shook rain off my coat and apologised for the intrusion'.   4/8

3. When the author first arrived in North Uist he wasn't at all keen on the place. It was a 'watery nightmare', ✓

Writing to analyse, review, comment

26

Good textual support.

not a welcoming place we can see this in the text:
'inhospitable landscape'. Another thing what he didn't really
like about North Uist was the smell: which we can also see
in the text: 'I was immediately aware of that smell which
was to become too familiar. A compound of seaweed and rain
and peat-smoke, acid and invigorating ✓ and mixed with the
universal hill-farm smell of sheep.'

However, when he stopped to ask for further directions
the people were so friendly, inviting him in and wanting to
know all about him. They were not in the slightest bit angry
with him for him turning up on their doorstep all of a
sudden. ✓

Good concluding point.

In the end I think the author enjoyed his holiday to
North Uist. He wasn't sure at the beginning, but as soon
as he met the people he changed his mind.   5/8

Total 14/25

Grade booster ┄┄⟩ move C to B

- Good points are made here but more development of them is needed.
- More detailed comment and analysis of the points made.

GRADE A ANSWER

Andrew

1. After reading this article, I came to a quite
obvious conclusion that the island of Uist is a
very hilly, rural, area. Apart from the unfamiliar
terrain that the author said was confusing, he
also states that 'No map could give a true
impression of the landscape'. ✓ This may well be
true but in words he goes on to create a visual
image of this wild and desolate island. 'Between
areas of water were strips of heather and moor
grasses shrunken by strong wind ✓ and into
everything rain poured down', which indicates to
me that it is a very wet, maybe even boggy
green land. At the end of line 27, the author
uses a metaphor with the words 'watery
nightmare'; ✓ this is also another good example
of the island's weather conditions. When the
author stops to ask for directions he is invited
into an old man's house because the winds are so
strong they cannot introduce themselves to one
another stood on his doorstep. The people on the

Clear and focused opening – good points, well put.

Good textual support.

Specific references and identification of language use.

GRADE A ANSWER

Evaluation taking place here.

island must be very trusting, as well as sincere to invite a stranger in off the road and into their own home. ✓ I would imagine that it is a very hospitable, inviting island or that at least is the impression the author creates in my mind. ✓   7/8

Good summary, using evidence to draw conclusions.

2. The lifestyle of the inhabitants I would say is a very relaxed, traditional, hard working one. The old man that the author meets says not to worry about being late for Murdo Iain Macdonald of Glebe because he will be expecting him at any time. ✓ The old man says that they are all called Macdonald on the island and Murdo is a second cousin of his. The old man knows how to get everywhere on the island and proves this by telling the author exactly how to get to Murdo Macdonald's household with 'clear directions'. He does this 'in his own good time' though which further suggests an unhurried ✓ and tranquil approach to life in general. I would say that the entire population of Uist Island know each other and that they live in a very harmonious and tight-knit community. ✓   6/8

Relevant textual references to support points.

Perceptive point.

Support would help here.

3. The author uses descriptive language quite a lot but at the beginning of the article it is factual, here he talks about the size of the island and the distance between getting off the ferry and arriving at his destination. Then he uses descriptive language like 'the sheer ✓ unfamiliarity of the terrain was confusing'. He states that the landscape was inhospitable, and goes for a negative angle and probably feels depressed that he has gone to a windy, rainy island. In the latter end of the article it appears that the author has taken a bit more of a liking to the island and shows this with words like 'sincere', 'inviting' and 'gentle amusement', ✓ when he meets the old man and asks for directions.   7/9

Specific comments on language being made here.

Total 20/25

Grade booster ⤳ move A to A*
- Some ideas could be developed in a little more detail.
- More textual support for one or two points would be helpful.

1 Read the following extract which is taken from *My Family and Other Animals*, in which the author describes his family as they decide to leave England to go and live on the Greek island of Corfu. When you have finished your reading, answer the questions which follow. You should spend about 45 minutes on this question.

The Migration

July had been blown out like a candle by a biting wind that ushered in a leaden August sky. A sharp, stinging drizzle fell, billowing into opaque grey sheets when the wind caught it. Along the Bournemouth sea-front the beach-huts turned blank wooden faces towards a greeny-grey, froth-chained sea that leapt eagerly at the cement bulwark of the shore. The gulls had been tumbled inland over the town, and they now drifted above the house-tops on taut wings, whining peevishly. It was the sort of weather calculated to try anyone's endurance.

Considered as a group my family was not a very prepossessing sight that afternoon, for the weather had brought with it the usual selection of ills to which we were prone. For me, lying on the floor, labelling my collection of shells, it had brought catarrh, pouring it into my skull like cement, so that I was forced to breathe stertorously through open mouth. For my brother Leslie, hunched dark and glowering by the fire, it had inflamed the convolutions of his ears so that they bled delicately but persistently. To my sister Margo it had delivered a fresh dappling of acne spots to a face that was already blotched like a red veil. For my mother there was a rich, bubbling cold, and a twinge of rheumatism to season it. Only my eldest brother, Larry, was untouched, but it was sufficient that he was irritated by our failings.

It was Larry, of course, who started it. The rest of us felt too apathetic to think of anything except our own ills, but Larry was designed by Providence to go through life like a small, blond firework, exploding ideas in other people's minds, and then curling up with cat-like unctuousness and refusing to take any blame for the consequences. He had become increasingly irritable as the afternoon wore on. At length, glancing moodily round the room, he decided to attack Mother, as being the obvious cause of the trouble.

'Why do we stand this bloody climate?' he asked suddenly, making a gesture towards the rain-distorted window. 'Look at it! And, if it comes to that, look at us…Margo swollen up like a plate of scarlet porridge…Leslie wandering around with fourteen fathoms of cotton wool in each ear…Gerry sounds as though he's had a cleft palate from birth…And look at you: you're looking more decrepit and hag-ridden every day.'

Mother peered over the top of a large volume entitled *Easy Recipes from Rajputana*.

'Indeed I'm not,' she said indignantly.

'You *are*,' Larry insisted; 'you're beginning to look like an Irish washerwoman…and your family looks like a series of illustrations from a medical encyclopaedia.'

Mother could think of no really crushing reply to this, so she contented herself with a glare before retreating once more behind her book.

'What we need is sunshine,' Larry continued; 'don't you agree, Les?…Les…*Les!*'

Leslie unravelled a large quantity of cotton wool from one ear.

'What d'you say?' he asked.

'There you are!' said Larry, turning triumphantly to Mother, 'it's become a major operation to hold a conversation with him. I ask you, what a position to be in! One brother can't hear what you say, and the other one can't be understood. Really, it's time something was done. I can't be expected to produce deathless prose in an atmosphere of gloom and eucalyptus.'

'Yes dear,' said Mother vaguely.

'What we all need,' said Larry, getting into his stride again, 'is sunshine…a country where we can *grow*.'

'Yes, dear, that would be nice,' agreed Mother, not really listening.

'I had a letter from George this morning – he says Corfu's wonderful. Why don't we pack up and go to Greece?'

'Very well, dear, if you like,' said Mother unguardedly.

Where Larry was concerned she was generally very careful not to commit herself.

'When?' asked Larry, rather surprised at this cooperation.

Mother, perceiving that she had made a tactical error, cautiously lowered *Easy Recipes from Rajputana*.

'Well, I think it would be a sensible idea if you were to go on ahead, dear, and arrange things. Then you can write and tell me if it's nice, and we all can follow,' she said cleverly.

Larry gave her a withering look.

'You said *that* when I suggested going to Spain,' he reminded her, 'and I sat for two interminable months in Seville, waiting for you to come out, while you did nothing except write me massive letters about drains and drinking-water, as though I was the Town Clerk or something. No, if we're going to Greece, let's all go together.'

'You do *exaggerate*, Larry,' said Mother plaintively; 'anyway, I can't go just like that. I have to arrange something about this house.'

'Arrange? Arrange what, for heaven's sake? Sell it.'

'I can't do that, dear,' said Mother, shocked.

'Why not?'

'But I've only just bought it.'

'Sell it while it's still untarnished, then.'

'Don't be ridiculous, dear,' said Mother firmly; 'that's quite out of the question. It would be madness.'

So we sold the house and fled from the gloom of the English summer, like a flock of migrating swallows.

We all travelled light, taking with us only what we considered to be the bare essentials of life. When we opened our luggage for Customs inspection, the contents of our bags were a fair indication of character and interests. Thus Margo's luggage contained a multitude of diaphanous garments, three books on slimming, and a regiment of small bottles each containing some elixir guaranteed to cure acne. Leslie's case held a couple of roll-top pullovers and a pair of trousers which were wrapped round two revolvers, an air-pistol, a book called *Be Your Own Gunsmith*, and a large bottle of oil that leaked. Larry was accompanied by two trunks of books and a brief-case containing his clothes. Mother's luggage was sensibly divided between clothes and various volumes on cooking and gardening. I travelled with only those items that I thought necessary to relieve the tedium of a long journey: four books on natural history, a butterfly net, a dog, and a jam-jar full of caterpillars all in imminent danger of turning into chrysalids. Thus, by our standards fully equipped, we left the clammy shores of England.

from My Family and Other Animals *by Gerald Durrell*

a) How does the writer convey an impression of the English weather in the first four paragraphs? Use specific details from the text to support your ideas. ⑧

b) Examine the ways in which the writer uses details of the family's luggage in the final paragraph to reflect each character's individual interests. ⑧

c) Analyse the ways in which the writer uses language to convey an impression of Larry and Mother. You should use specific details from the text to support your ideas. ⑨

TOTAL 25

2 Read the following article from a magazine for people who are interested in writing. When you have finished your reading answer the questions which follow. You should spend about 45 minutes on this section.

Freelance Writing

The complete beginners column

Starting a new series for beginner writers

So you want to be a writer? What is more you have a brand new pad of paper, and your pen is poised to start writing. But writing what?

Before we address that question, do remember one thing: you are to be congratulated on having got this far. The world is full of people who say that, one day, they are going to write – but most of them never get round to it. For many would-be writers, it all remains a daydream. You, however, have at least started.

Having made that much effort, you must now understand that discipline is all important. The only way to write is to sit yourself down and to get on with it – and to do so regularly and consistently. Unless you discipline yourself to make writing a regular habit, your writing career is soon going to hit the buffers. It is not the slightest use waiting for inspiration to strike, waiting until you feel in the mood, waiting until you have lots of wonderful ideas to write about. Start the waiting game and in ten years' time you will still be waiting.

If, on the other hand, you discipline yourself to sit down to your writing every day, then the inspiration will eventually come, the ideas will begin to flow. So lesson number one is simple enough, but absolutely vital: set aside a given period of time, ideally every day but less frequently if you genuinely do not have time, and make sure that you are at your desk at that time as regular as clockwork. At some of these writing sessions the words will simply not flow, but even so you must be disciplined enough to write something. Write the opening paragraph for a magazine article, a short story opening, anything, but do not take the easy option and simple knock off for a cup of coffee. Knocking off for a cup of coffee can become a habit, and the habit you really need to acquire is that of writing.

Most successful writers will tell you that they have to discipline themselves to sit down every day and to write

whether they feel like it or not. Some set themselves targets, perhaps to achieve 1,000 words, perhaps more, perhaps less. If this all sounds like hard work – it is. No one ever said that writing was easy. But being hard work is not the same as being a chore. Although you

have to make yourself sit down, and some days make yourself write, it should still be a fascinating and enjoyable challenge. If it is not, then writing is simply not for you; if you do not enjoy it, you will never be good at it.

Having understood the need for discipline, you must then accept that you will need to learn your craft as a writer. Had you taken up music, or painting, or snooker, you would accept the need to learn skills of that particular activity. For some reason, however, many people think that they can sit down and write a bestseller straight away. No problem. They have this great idea, and all they need to do is knock it into words.

It is, of course, perfectly true that some people have indeed sat down and written a successful novel straight away. But do not be seduced by stories of people who became successful writers without any experience of the business and without any training. Few writers achieve immediate success, and those who do usually know something of the publishing or communications business. They know enough to be able to judge what would have popular appeal, and they know enough to ensure that their manuscript finds its way to an editor's desk somewhere.

Their alleged lack of training is also beguilingly misleading. Most successful

writers will be people who read extensively and who absorb what they are reading. And there can be no better training for a writer than to absorb published material. The advice from many successful authors is one simple word: Read. Read everything you can get your hands on. Read books, magazines, cereal packets, anything that comes your way. And absorb the way the sentences are crafted, the paragraphs constructed, the pace varied, the ideas linked together. If you can develop a feel for writing technique in this way, then you are well on the way to developing your own – and saleable – writing.

Having said there can be no better training than reading, let us recognise that there is one good form of training that is equally good: Writing. The more you write, the more skilled you become at it, and the more quickly will you develop your own style and tone of voice. This is particularly true if you combine regular, analytical, reading with your regular disciplined writing.

Accepting that you should therefore sit down and get on with your writing, we come back to the question we started with: Writing what? One of the best answers is that you should start by writing for your local newspaper. There are dozens of local organisations that would welcome the help of someone willing to become press officer. It may be the local horticultural society, the local rugby club, the Women's Institute. They will all have hard pressed committees, and will be delighted if you come forward with the offer to write press reports of their activities for submission to the local newspaper.

You will not, of course, be paid for this. Local societies rely on voluntary help, and local newspapers do not pay for news reports. But you will gain huge non-monetary rewards: you will be practising your writing skills, you will have the disciplines of deadlines and copy dates, you will be seeing your work appear in print.

And when it does appear in print, be sure to cut it out and keep it. At least that way you are beginning to build your own cutting file.

Writing Magazine December 1995–January 1996

Writing to analyse, review, comment

a) What advice is offered to would-be writers in the first four paragraphs of the article? ⑧

b) What suggestions are made as to how potential writers can begin to learn the craft of writing in paragraphs 5–9? ⑦

c) Analyse the ways in which the writer uses language to convey information and ideas effectively. How successful do you find the article? ⑩

TOTAL 25

1 a) The writer wishes to convey a sense of the poor weather that can occur in England. His description is made all the more effective because the month is August, a time when we might expect good weather – but not, apparently, in England. He uses imagery to make his description both vivid and funny. Here are some examples:

- The simile of July being 'blown out like a candle by a biting wind'.
- The description of the August sky as 'leaden' giving an impression of the dark grey sky.
- The 'opaque grey sheets of drizzle'.
- The drizzle described as 'sharp' and 'stinging'
- The rough grey sea, 'a greeny-grey, froth-chained sea that leapt eagerly at the cement bulwark of the shore' (note the personification here).
- The gulls being blown in the wind catching the dismal mood by 'whining peevishly'.
- The various illnesses that the poor weather had brought to the family.
- The 'rain-distorted window'.

b)
- Margot's luggage reflects her concern with her appearance, her liking for 'diaphanous garments', the books on slimming and the acne cures.
- Leslie's luggage contains few clothes but has two revolvers and an air-pistol, the oil to maintain them and a book entitled *Be Your Own Gunsmith*, all of which reflect his interest in guns and shooting.
- Larry's enthusiasm for books and reading and lack of interest in personal appearance is seen through his luggage consisting of two trunks of books and only a brief-case containing his clothes.
- The writer's possessions show his passion for natural history and animals – four books on natural history, a butterfly net, a dog and a jar of caterpillars.

c) The basic point here is that Larry is the dominant character who takes the lead while Mother tries to please everyone and keep them all happy.

Larry:
- 'It was Larry, of course, who started it.'
- 'Larry was designed by Providence to go through life like a small, blond firework, exploding ideas into other people's minds.'
- His forceful manner of introducing the idea of going abroad to live – 'Why do we stand this bloody climate?' etc.
- His insistent manner.
- His technique of using exaggeration to press his point.

Mother:
- Her mild nature – e.g. 'she contented herself with a glare before retreating once more behind her book'.
- Her vague, non-committal responses to Larry's suggestions, '"Yes dear," said Mother vaguely.' '"Yes dear, that would be nice," agreed Mother, not really listening.'
- What happens is precisely the opposite to what she had said – e.g. '"that's quite out of the question."...So we sold the house...'.

EXAMINER'S TIP

*Make sure that you use plenty of specific detail from the text to support the points you make. Remember – on these kinds of questions you should be analysing **HOW** the writer uses language, not simply describing what is said.*

2 a)
- Sit down and write regularly.
- Set aside a period of time each day or as often as you can to write.
- Self-discipline is needed.
- Get something down on paper even if you are not inspired.
- Set yourself a target of writing so many words each session.
- Enjoy it.
- Do not just give up and have a coffee break if you cannot think of anything to write.
- Be aware that writing is hard work.

b)
- Learn about the publishing business.
- Read extensively.
- Absorb what you read.
- Look at the ways in which writing is contrasted (ideas, pace, etc.)
- Develop a feel for writing techniques.
- Develop your own writing style.
- Write as regularly as you can.
- Read regularly and analytically.
- Try writing for your local newspaper.
- Try offering your services as a press officer.

c)
- The use of the rhetorical question in the first paragraph involves the reader immediately and gives them questions they will see answered in the article.
- The use of 'you' also makes the piece more personal, directed at the reader and makes them feel involved.
- The vocabulary is straightforward, clear and easy to understand.
- Key points are stressed using strong positive language – 'absolutely vital', 'successful writers', 'read extensively'.
- Specific groups and bodies are mentioned – 'local rugby club', 'Women's Institute'.
- You need to evaluate how successful you find the article – the main thing is to give reasons for your comments.

Writing to analyse, review, comment

CHAPTER 4

Writing to inform, explain, describe

To revise this topic more thoroughly, see Chapter 4 in Letts *Revise GCSE English Study Guide.*

 Try this sample GCSE question and then compare your answer with the Grade C and Grade A model answers on pages 35–37.

Spend about 45 minutes on this question.

Remember:

*   spend 10 minutes planning and sequencing your material
*   write about 300–400 words
*   spend 10 minutes checking:

    your paragraphing

    your punctuation

    your spelling.

You are organising a visit for your class to a major museum in a city of your choice. Write an information sheet for students going on the visit informing them of the arrangements and procedures to be followed on the visit.

You might write about:

*   the travel arrangements to and from the city
*   the programme of activities to be followed in the museum
*   eating arrangements
*   conduct and behaviour.

(25 marks)

GRADE C ANSWER

Sharon

A Visit to a Museum

We are going by coach to Cardiff Museum. So for those of you who are interested, would you please bring your letters of consent along with £8.00 on the day – or otherwise you will not be let onto the coach.

You will need to have a lunch box with your lunch inside and a drink – Please Note, there should be NO glass bottles! And no eating on the coach.

We will meet at 9.00am outside the school and the ✓ coach will arrive at 9.15am. The coach will leave the school at 9.30am, which by then we will be all settled on the coach.

There will be two children to a seat and your name will be called out. There will be some staff and helpers, which when your name is called out you will be appointed to for the duration of the journey.

We will stop for a ten minute break at a service area and you should stay with your appointed adult during that ✓ time. From there we will go back on the coach and should arrive at Cardiff at 10.45 am. After getting off the coach you will line up in pairs and walk to the museum.

Once we get to the museum and we go in you should stay with your appointed adult all the time. We have allowed two hours to look round the museum and then we will have lunch at about 1.00pm. ✓

The coach will be picking us up at half past one. So we need to be ready by then.

Sick bags will be available on the coach if anyone feels ill. If you do feel ill then let your appointed adult know straight away. We will also have a first aid kit in case anyone is injured.

We will arrive back in Bristol at around 2.30pm and so your parents will need to be back at the school by that time in order to pick you up.

14/25

Clear but could be phrased more effectively.

Clear information given.

The message is clear but expression could be improved.

Once again, detailed and clear information.

More details are given here.

Overall clear information is given here with attention paid to detail.

Grade booster ····} move C to B

- Some of the points could be expressed more effectively.
- The structure of the piece could be improved to make the points more clearly – perhaps bullet points might help here.

GRADE A ANSWER

Andrew

All Students

Good, clear opening. Needs to check phasing though.

Please be aware of the up coming trip to the Tate Art Gallery, London. This trip is primarily intended for those students who are ✓ studying an art or culture based course, but any spare spaces will be available to other students. This trip is to take place on Thursday 4th May, and is usually a very popular outing, so please book your place early so as to avoid dissappointment. ✓

Effectively put points.

We shall be travelling down to London by train as though this type of transport will increase the cost of the trip slightly, it shall also ensure the maximum amount of time possible will be spent in London. The train will be leaving Nottingham Station at ✓ 8.45am. Students are asked to make their own way to the station and to be there fifteen minutes before departure i.e. 8.30am. We will all meet outside W.H.Smith promptley.

Clear and thorough points made with attention to detail.

The cost of the trip will be £47. This price includes the cost of the return train ticket and also entry to the Art Gallery. Please note you must have your student I.D. on your person as the Art Gallery may require to see them. Students are advised that an extra £3 will be required on the day to purchase tube tickets as this is not included in the cost of the trip. Also any personal spending money should be taken if required. ✓

The whole purpose of this trip is to give students an idea of the different types of art that can be displayed in a gallery format. To enable yourselves to get the maximum benefit from the day a series of activities and events have been planned, these are as follows. The group will arrive at the gallery at approximately 10.30am and will be met by our guide for the day. The guide will start off by

A good deal of information here clearly explained.

SPELLCHECK!

upcoming
primarily
disappointment
it will
promptly

taking us to the guest room. Here we shall be given a short talk of the history of the art gallery and watch a short video introducing us to the gallery. All this should last around thirty minutes. From there we will then be given a guided tour of two of the gallery's exhibitions. The idea behind having a guided tour is so there will always be somebody on hand to answer your questions. They will also be asking you questions too. ✓

At around 1.30pm we will break for lunch. It is advisable to take some kind of packed lunch as food can often be expensive at the gallery. After lunch you will be allowed to look around two more of the gallery's exhibitions for yourselves. At 3.30 we shall then all meet up at the guest room, where each student will be asked a question on the exhibitions that they have been looking at in the afternoon, so pay attention on your way round. ✓

Very detailed information given with attention paid to every aspect of the trip.

At all times during this trip all of the college's codes of conduct must be adeared to. Any students found breaking these codes shall be disciplnned.

We will be departing London St. Pancras Satation at 4.35pm and will arrive back at Nottingham at 6.02pm. Those students interested in this trip should complete the slip below and return it with a £15 deposit to the college office no later than Friday 28th April. ✓

Overall very thorough with a good deal of essential information clearly presented and explained.

22/25

Writing to inform, explain, describe

Grade booster ┅┅> move A to A*

- Some of the information could have been more easily conveyed through the use of bullet points.
- Attention should be paid to technical accuracy here, particularly spelling.

Writing to inform, explain, describe

You should spend about 45 minutes on each question.

Remember – you should:

- spend 10 minutes planning and sequencing your material
- write about 300–400 words
- spend 10 minutes checking:

  your paragraphing

  your punctuation

  your spelling.

Each question carries **25 marks**

1 Describe the scene in a town centre on a Saturday afternoon.

You should write about one to two pages. Remember that this is a test of your ability to write descriptively.

2 Describe a personal experience that still really sticks in your mind.

3 Describe an aeroplane flight, a long car or train journey or a sea crossing.

4 Imagine that you are giving a class talk in which you explain the procedures that you need to go through to

a) join a club or society **OR**

b) prepare for an overseas holiday **OR**

c) apply for a part-time job.

5 Explain how you felt at an important moment in your life.

6 You are responsible for organising your school play this year and need to write an information leaflet/poster giving full details of the production and asking for volunteers. The leaflet will be displayed on key notice boards in school and copies will be sent to parents. Write the leaflet.

You might include the following information:

- which play is being performed and the various parts which will be allocated
- details of audition dates/times, etc.
- requests for volunteers for various 'backstage' jobs
- dates and venue for performance
- any other information that you think is required.

7 Write a description of a person you admire. You might include details such as:

- appearance
- how they behave
- why you admire them
- any other details you find important.

8 Write about your ambition for the future, explaining how and why you have made your choices.

9   You have been invited to attend an interview for a job that you really want. Explain what you would do to prepare yourself for the interview.

Here are some points you might think about:

- preparation for possible questions
- personal appearance
- conduct at the interview
- getting to the venue
- any other points you think important.

10   Write a description of a party you have held, or that has been held for you or one that you have been to.

11   Read the following article in which the singer/songwriter, Errol Brown describes his life and people who influenced him at various points.

Write a short description of your own life focusing on one or two people who have had an important influence on you.

My best teacher Errol Brown

I was born in Kingston, in Jamaica, and I went to a primary school like any other over there – very strict. You had to be smart, and you got punished when you stepped out of line. Then, when I was 11, we moved to London and I went to a secondary modern in Streatham, near Crystal Palace. It was so long ago I don't even remember the name of it.

When I was 14, we moved from that part of the world to West Hampstead, and my mother – who was my greatest inspiration – sent me to Warwick House private school, which was Jewish but had other religions. That was the major move in my life because secondary moderns didn't encourage you to have any ambitions at all beyond being a manual worker. They made out that you didn't have the brain power. Everyone in Streatham wanted to be a bus driver or a plumber, but when I went to the private school, everyone wanted to be doctors, lawyers and accountants. There was a completely different mindset about what you could achieve in your life, and how you could better yourself.

I liked Latin for some reason, and it is the Latin teacher from Warwick House who sticks in my mind. He was a very

big guy, probably in his mid-30s, and he looked like a Roman warrior. He was from Athens and his name actually was Mr Athens. I'll always remember him because he was a lovely teacher but he had a terrible temper. When we started talking in class he would bite his lip – and that's when you knew you had to watch it. Then he was right behind you, before you knew it, twisting your ear.

He was a great teacher, though. Latin can be very dull, but he encouraged you and made lessons very interesting. He got you involved and made you feel good if you got things right. It was over 30 years ago but I can still remember how pleasant he was. He got me motivated to do well, but I still lacked direction at that age.

I wanted to be an engineer even though I had no feel for it, and then I went to business school but I didn't want to be a businessman. Even though I enjoyed music and danced in clubs, I never saw myself as a music maker until I was 20. It was a friend of mine, Tony Wilson, who was the big influence in my music.

I would go tenpin bowling with Tony, and I used to have these melodies in my head and these words would come out in the car. At that stage, the only experience I'd had singing was in the school choir but, being a songwriter, he recognised how catchy my melodies were. He said: "Why don't you come and write songs with me?" I was amazed. I didn't think I could do it but that's basically how I came into it, and from there we went on to co-found Hot Chocolate. Tony left the band in 1976 to go solo in America, but unfortunately it didn't work out for him and I think he ended up in Trinidad, where he was born.

I haven't seen him since 1976 because we fell out, unfortunately – it was one of those things about different music directions.

I never saw myself becoming a pop star, but that was my destiny. I had all these ambitions that were way above me and I was never comfortable. I was always searching so I would pluck these things out of the air that I wanted to be, but I was never really interested enough in what I was studying to make it in those areas. Eventually I discovered my real ability – and that was writing songs.

Singer Errol Brown was talking to John Guy.

THE STORY SO FAR

1948 Born in Jamaica
1959 Moves to London
1963 Warwick House School, West Hampstead
1967 Sits A-levels
1969 Lead singer of Hot Chocolate, which he co-founds with Tony Wilson
1970 Debut single, 'Love is Life', reaches number 6 in the UK charts. String of hits follows including 'Emma', 'It Started with a Kiss' and 'Everyone's a Winner'
1981 Performs at Prince Charles and Princess Diana's wedding reception
1985 Leaves Hot Chocolate
1990 Relaunches his career with solo UK tour
1997 The 1975 hit, 'You Sexy Thing', is revived in the film *The Full Monty*
2001 Tours to promote his album, Still Sexy
2002 New single due out

12 Write an informative article for your school magazine in which you describe and explain a favourite hobby or interest that you have.

13 Places can look very different in different circumstances. Choose **one** of the following and write a description of it before and after the event:

- A street before and after a street party
- Your classroom before and after a class
- Your lounge before and after you have held a party for your friends
- A carnival ground while the carnival is on and after it has finished
- A holiday resort seafront while everything is open and after everything has closed for the night.

14 Describe your ideal home.

15 Explain your views on a topic or issue that you feel strongly about.

QUESTION BANK ANSWERS

EXAMINER'S TIP

General advice
The kinds of questions that come under the general heading of 'inform, explain, describe' can be very varied as you will have seen from the Question Bank questions. They do not have 'right' or 'wrong' answers and very often they can be approached in many different ways. Here are some general points to bear in mind.

- *Be clear in your mind about the purpose of your writing and the audience you are addressing.*
- *Use an appropriate register and vocabulary.*
- *Write in well-structured sentences and make sure that your spelling and punctuation are accurate.*
- *If you are 'informing' or 'explaining' make sure that your information is presented clearly and logically.*
- *If the main intention is to describe, make your description as vivid as possible but without going 'over the top'.*
- *Present your work well.*

1
- The description should be specific to a town centre on a Saturday afternoon.
- You should try to focus on specific details and describe them as vividly as possible but without being over-extravagant in your use of language.
- The use of adjectives, adverbs and imagery, particularly the use of metaphors and similes, can help to make your description more vivid.

2
- Careful selection of the experience is important here.
- Building up the background to the experience can help to make it more vivid.
- Well-chosen vocabulary will make the description more effective.

3
- Description based on personal experience can help to make your writing more vivid and convincing.
- Your work should focus on the vivid description of the experience.
- Small details can help to bring your writing to life and make it more 'real' to the reader.

4
- Your response should use language appropriate to a class talk.
- You should select your option carefully and your talk should focus closely on that choice.

- Your writing should explain the procedures clearly and logically.

EXAMINER'S TIP

Remember that you are preparing a talk and that it is to be spoken rather than read, so use language appropriately.

5
- The careful selection of your topic is very important here.
- Your writing should give a real sense of the experience to your reader, so it is important to refer to details of what you thought, and how you responded to events.
- You should focus particularly on how you felt, as that is what the question asks you to do.

6
- You should include the name of the play and preferably a brief indication of the kind of play it is.
- You should be specific about the various roles you are asking for volunteers for, perhaps including a brief description of what is involved in each job.
- The information should be clear and include all the necessary details.

7
- Your description should focus on specific details.
- You should describe why you admire your chosen person.
- Your work should be structured clearly.

8
- Your ideas should focus on 'ambition', although this can be interpreted in as wide a sense as you wish and need not be confined to a 'job' or 'career'.
- Explain your choice(s) and give reasons for them.
- Your work should be structured clearly.

9
- You should be specific about the job you are going to be interviewed for.
- Your writing should cover the full range of preparations you might make for it.
- You might organise your work under sub-headings to make the points more clearly.

EXAMINER'S TIP

Don't forget basic details such as how to get to the venue and making sure you are on time, as well as the important area of preparing your ideas for the interview.

10
- You should specify the kind of party you are

writing about and how it came to be held.

- Your writing should convey a vivid sense of the party and capture the atmosphere.
- You should focus on descriptions of both people and surroundings.

EXAMINER'S TIP

Make sure that you pay close attention to the specific terms of the question that you are answering and focus on giving the information required, explaining clearly or describing as required. Do beware of being overly descriptive, though. It is easy to 'go over the top' when writing descriptively.

⑪
- Your description should focus on specific details.
- You should focus on one or two people who have had an important influence on you.
- You should select your ideas carefully – focus on a small number of key points.
- Your work should be structured clearly.

EXAMINER'S TIP

Do not become involved in long drawn out explanations or descriptions of your life. Be concise and keep your writing focused and sharp.

⑫
- Your response should use language appropriate to a school magazine.
- You should select your topic carefully and your article should focus closely on that choice.
- Your writing should explain how you became interested in the hobby and what appeals to you about it.

⑬
- Description based on personal experience can help to make your writing more vivid and convincing.
- Your work should focus on the vivid description of the chosen topic.
- Your description should bring out the contrasts of the two circumstances.
- Small details can help to bring your writing to life and make it more real to the reader.

EXAMINER'S TIP

Make sure that you pay close attention to the specific terms of the question that you are answering and focus on giving the information required, explaining clearly or describing as required. Do beware of being overly descriptive, though. It is easy to 'go over the top' when writing descriptively.

⑭
- Your description should focus on specific details.
- You should describe why you would look for certain features in your 'ideal' home.
- Your work should be structured clearly.

⑮
- Careful selection of topic is important here.
- Make sure that you have plenty of ideas.
- It should be a topic that you feel strongly about.
- Explain your ideas clearly.

FOR MORE INFORMATION ON THIS TOPIC ... SEE REVISE GCSE ENGLISH ... CHAPTER 4

CHAPTER 5

Writing on media texts

To revise this topic more thoroughly, see Chapter 5 in Letts *Revise GCSE English Study Guide*.

 Try this sample GCSE question and then compare your answer with the Grade C and Grade A model answers on pages 46–48.

Read the article 'The Petrifying Truth' which was published in *The Big Issue in the North*.

Answer **both** parts of the question.

a   Summarise the ideas that the writer wants to convey to his readers in this article. **[10]**

b   Examine the ways in which the writer communicates the various ideas in the article.

Comment on how effective you found it overall.   **[15]**

In your answer you should comment on:

- the content of the article
- the use of headlines, pictures and diagrams
- any other features related to layout and design
- the use of language
- the different views offered.

(Total 25 marks)

THE PETRIFYING TRUTH

NEVER MIND THE GERMANS, IF YOU GO TO YORKSHIRE BEACHES THIS SUMMER, REMEMBER THE DINOSAURS WERE THERE FIRST, SAYS **DAVE WINDASS**. ILLUSTRATION BY **DANIEL COOKNEY**

Come the sunshine and Yorkshire's beautiful coast draws three million visitors every year.

But few realise, as they struggle with the deckchairs and sandy sarnies, they are sharing their sunbathing spot with the remains of what were once the most awesome land animals ever to walk the earth.

Yet the evidence is all around them. From the small fishing village inlet of Staithes down to the seaside resort of Filey, there is a treasure trove of fossils bringing the lives – and deaths – of the dinosaurs vividly to life.

> "FOSSILS ARE THE FRAGILE END OF THINGS. PEOPLE THINK THAT THEY ARE AN INFINITE RESOURCE YOU CAN BASH THE HELL OUT OF BUT THEY'RE NOT"

Stroll along the coastline and you could be literally standing on the shoulders of giants.

Sadly it is this accessibility which has, over the last couple of centuries, led to a serious depletion of fossil stocks, something the newly-founded Yorkshire Dinosaur Coast Project is keen to halt.

But project officer, Alistair Bowden hopes common sense will prevail before the need for legal restraint.

"We don't want to be killjoys at all," he says. "If there's a fossil that is [already] out of the rock, that's going to be destroyed by the sea, I'd much rather someone had it."

"I have had a lot of joy out of collecting fossils, that's how I started, that's how a lot of people start and I don't want to stop that."

The project, a partnership between the museums of Scarborough, Whitby, Yorkshire and Humberside and the North York Moors National Park, was officially launched in the shadows of the sandstone cliffs of Scarborough. As an event it promised to be rather a fusty scientific affair.

While there were a large number of experts wearing the requisite hiking boots, khaki shorts and cardigans, for five hours of hands-on activity, people from 32 different organisations did their best to convey the excitement and passion they feel for fossils, rocks and all things dinosaur.

Palaeontologist, Phil Manning, is the Yorkshire Museum's Keeper of Geology and an advisor on the BBC's recent high-profile series, *Walking With Dinosaurs*. Partly responsible for informing our views on the giant prehistoric creatures – and correcting the Velociraptor mistakes Steven Spielberg made in *Jurassic Park* – Manning insists science should always be fun.

Which is why we end up sculpting dinosaurs out of sand on Scarborough beach, indulging the peculiar art of fossil rubbing and finish the day with trouser-legs rolled up, standing in a rock pool.

Behind the fun and prehistoric education there is, of course, a serious issue – protecting the fossil resource by encouraging people not to take the fossils home as souvenirs.

"We've got to tell people that this coast is internationally important, it's exceptional, it's marvellous, it's really interesting. And then they may think, 'Aha, we shouldn't be bashing it with hammers'," says Bowden, "maybe we should be going along taking photographs, sketching things and leaving it for others to see".

"The fossils are the fragile end of things. People think that they are an infinite resource you can bash the hell out of but they're not."

All somewhat different to life in the lower Jurassic period of 205 million years ago – when this land mass was a little nearer the equator and marine reptiles like Ichthyosaurs and Plesiosaurs found themselves swimming alongside belemnites and ammonites. Or the tropical rain forest conditions of the mid-Jurassic when huge land-living *Sauropoda* dinosaurs like Diplodocus and Brachiosaurus were chomping on the lush, readily available vegetation – huge ferns and 100ft monkey puzzle trees. For a while the area resembled the Ganges.

The unwritten code of fossil collecting suggests if it's in a rock, leave it. It is with genuine dismay Bowden recalls amateurs' ham-fisted efforts to take dinosaur footprints home as trophies.

"I've seen footprints destroyed when people have tried to take them out with a hammer and that's it, you can't see them anymore – all you can see is the crack but you know they've destroyed it. It's a shame – they've failed to get a nice fossil and everyone else has lost it."

The project aims to raise understanding among those people who are rather more concerned with the prom, chips and ice cream than the history and exceptional geological heritage of Yorkshire's coast.

Though it is rare to discover a completely fossilised dinosaur, an ancestor of Brachiosaurus was found in Scarborough in the 1820s, when both Scarborough and Whitby were at the real hub of the science of geology. However, these 80 tons-plus creatures have left plenty of calling cards along the coast. If you know what you are looking for there are hundreds of them.

But it is lack of laws preventing people taking whatever they want and a long-standing tradition of fossil hunters cracking stone nodules apart which accounts for the dearth of fossils in some areas these days, particularly around Robin Hood's Bay.

But Manning insists better public under-standing is all that's needed: "The Yorkshire coast has a fabulous wealth of fossils, a wealth that has been excavated since the early part of the 19th century," he says.

"One thing close to my heart is everyone has a right to go out and hunt for fossils and it's wonderful, you should do it, it's good therapeutic stuff. Finding fossils, there's nothing like it in the world. For me it's a great kick to pick up a fossil that no human being has looked at in more than 100 to 180 million years. And thankfully in Britain we don't have any Draconian laws to stop us doing that."

So rather than bludgeoning history out of existence by inexpertly trying to chip out your own newly unearthed fragment of dino-belia, it's much better, urges Manning, to either take photographs or casts of the footprints, leaving everything intact for future generations to enjoy.

Otherwise it may be us who prove to be the real dinosaurs one day.

For further information visit
www.dinocoast.org.uk

These two answers are at grades C and A. Compare which one your answer is closest to and think how you could have improved it.

GRADE C ANSWER

Tony

The Petrifying Truth

Good opening summary.

a. The article 'The Petrifying Truth' starts off with the writer explaining that 3 million people visit the East coast every year and most of them don't even know that they are sitting on a gold mine of fossils. The fossils stretch from Staithes right down to Filey and all of it tells a story of the life and death of the giant creatures that once lived. ✓

Some key details selected from article.

The fossils are extreamly easy to get to and it is this that has caused the number of fossils there to fall dramatically. The Yorkshire Dinosaur Coast Project is trying to stop this without having a law put on it. ✓ They don't mind people taking fossils that have already broken away but people shouldn't try to take them off the rocks because everybody should be able to see them without people trying to take them off the rocks and destroying them. Instead of trying to take the fossils home you should take photo's sketches and casts of the foot prints.

> **SPELLCHECK!**
>
> extremely
> photos
> exciting
> palaeontology
> were
> laid
> alliteration

Overall a good summary.

Fossil hunting is fun and exiting and it is very therapeutic instead of taking fossils they should be left for other generations to enjoy. ✓ **6/10**

A sense of personal voice but lacks closer focus on language and effects.

b. The article isn't very effective, it started off well with a gripping first paragraph that looks really interesting but it gradually goes off. To understand the article you have to have a specialist knowledge about paelentology, the writer does not explain enough for you to know what most of the big scientific words mean 'Sauropoda'.
The article isn't written very creatively, it's more like reading a text book than an article for the Big Issue. ✓
The large main title is very effective at getting you to look at the article. There was too many pictures all huddled together, it would have looked a lot better if there had only been a few well detailed pictures most of the pictures are a waste of space. The article is very poorly layed out because the two paragraphs at the top should not be away from the rest of the article.

Some relevant ideas.

Doesn't develop this idea at all.

The writer uses aliteration but this was the only good part of the language, it is too complex for people who do not have a degree in palaeontology. **8/15**

Total 14/25

> **Grade booster ⋯⟩ move C to B**
> • Ideas need developing more fully in terms of the ways in which language is used.
> • Spelling needs attention.

GRADE A ANSWER

Good summary that focuses on key ideas.

Clear sense of detail and understanding here.

Clear, well-structured writing covering the central points.

Although critical of the article there are a range of relevant ideas explored here.

Gemma

The Petrifying Truth

a. To summarise the above named article I would say that the writer first introduced us to the Yorkshire Dinosaur Coast Project a project set up to protect any and all fossils in and around the East Coast. ✓ The ideas that the writer wants to convey to his readers is that fossil hunting is fun, and you should read this article and want to go out and do it. Then it goes back 205 million years ago ✓ and gives you information all about 'Diplodocus and Brachiosaurs' and that they would be chomping on the '100ft lush monkey trees'. The writer gives a reason why you should go out and do it: because it is 'good therapeutic stuff' and then goes on to say what you must not do to the fossils. You must not try to remove them or keep them as a collectors item as they are there for everybody to see. At one point he even gives you a set of rules or a code to follow ✓ for collecting fossils adding that we should preserve fossils for future generations to see. The writer also includes and conveys some interesting information about dinosaurs and the period that they lived in. He also gives his opinion that fossil hunting is fun and that people should have a go and he asks Do not try to remove fossils take photographs and sketch things and leave it for others to see. ✓   8/10

b. The problems that I personally see with this article are it is not easy to understand unless you already have a understanding of fossils, he could have written the piece shorter and more to the point and he could have also been a bit more creative. ✓ I think that the piece was badly laid out and not really relevant for people who read the Big Issue. The content itself was also difficult to understand and was definitely written for

Doesn't really develop this idea.

a specific audience. However, it did start well in the first paragraph especially when using sibilance and did contain some general information and a few good points. The headlines, diagrams and pictures were very eye catching helping you to read more of the article instead of skimming through it. Also the writer also has a play on words (eg Petrifying) which has a double meaning. I feel that the illustrations tried to be too clever. I also did not like the way two columns of text were placed at the end of the headline giving the piece as a whole a kind of cluttered feel to it. However, on the plus side I think that the diagrams and such did ✓ relate to the article.

Strong personal voice and clear comments about language although reference to the text would be useful.

The use of language was also too complex and not well suited to the magazine the article was present in, it is more suited to the National Geographic and other magazines that include more articles like this. Again I will mention the use of double meaning words and also the use of alliteration. There was however a good use of imagery used in the 5th column, but again he used technical and scientific if not a kind of academic language. But I think the bit in the piece that really annoyed me was the corny language 'standing on the shoulders of giants'.

Clearly has a view on the text and makes some relevant evaluative comments. A personal voice and engagement here.

I think that this piece has mixed good and bad points but personally when I go to the east coast I won't be going out of my way ✓ to look for any fossils.   **13/15**

21/25

Grade booster ⇢ move A to A*
- More detailed development of some of the ideas.
- Closer focus on the language used with textual support to back up points.

QUESTION BANK

1 Read the article on page 50 'Penguins Die in Ice Limbo' from *The Sunday Times*. Answer **both** parts of the question.

a) Examine the ways in which the writer uses language to convey the key ideas to his readers. You should refer to specific examples of language use to support the points you make. ⑩

b) Comment on how effective you found the article overall. ⑮

   In your answer you should comment on:

   • the content of the article
   • the use of headlines, photographs and diagrams
   • any other features related to layout and design
   • the use of language
   • the different views offered.

TOTAL 25

Writing on media texts

ANSWERS ON PAGE 56 ANSWERS ON PAGE 56 ANSWERS ON PAGE 56 ANSWERS ON PAGE 56

'PENGUINS DIE IN ICE LIMBO'

Jonathan Leake
Science Editor

ANTARCTICA'S most important penguin colonies face disaster because a huge ice sheet has cut them off from their breeding grounds.

Hundreds of thousands of birds have been trapped at sea, forcing some to take refuge on ice floes. Many others are believed to have perished trying to cross the ice sheet to reach the breeding areas.

Scientists have considered a "pick up a penguin" rescue attempt similar to last year's airlift of 56,000 Jackass penguins from Dassen Island, off South Africa, after an oil spill.

Antarctic researchers have, however, ruled out a similar operation. "Picking up penguins from ice floes is impossible – they just dive into the water," said one.

The ice sheet has formed around two giant icebergs that grounded in the shallow waters near the penguin colonies. Satellite pictures show the sheet is 80 miles wide – up to four times bigger than normal.

The birds, which travel most efficiently through water, are used to walking only a few miles across ice from the open sea to their nests. But with a top waddling speed of only 1 mph the trip would take them nearly four days rather than the normal few hours. Tens of thousands are already believed to have starved to death.

Dr Keith Nicholls, of the British Antarctic Survey, described the destruction as a tragedy. "These are beautiful birds and their colonies are dependent on rearing chicks each year to replace those lost to the climate and predators," he said.

One of the colonies was discovered by Sir Ernest Shackleton, the explorer, during his 1914-17 voyage.

Pictures taken by a Nasa satellite gave the first warnings of the scale of disaster and American scientists at the McMurdo research station on Ross Island have since con-firmed it. The ice has cut off one of Antarctica's largest colonies of Adelie penguins from its breeding ground at Cape Crozier on Ross Island, which normally contains 250,000 birds. The birds are now stranded at sea and few are expected to reach the site. Another colony of Adelies trying to reach Cape Royds, also on Ross, is expected to "fail totally", while a third, containing 1,200 rare Emperor penguins, also at Cape Crozier has already been destroyed.

Scientists are deeply concerned. There are probably about 4m Adelie penguins across Antarctica. Emperor penguins are much rarer with only about 150,000 pairs left.

The icebergs that caused the disaster broke away from the edge of the Ross ice shelf in March 2000 and slowly drifted across the Ross Sea.

The scale of such ice

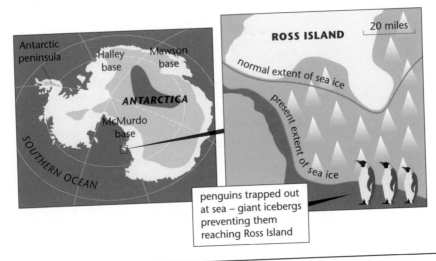

Antarctic peninsula | Halley base | Mawson base | ANTARCTICA | McMurdo base | SOUTHERN OCEAN

ROSS ISLAND | 20 miles | normal extent of sea ice | present extent of sea ice

penguins trapped out at sea – giant icebergs preventing them reaching Ross Island

movements is colossal. The Ross ice shelf is about the size of France; one of the icebergs it produced is 50 miles long and 20 miles wide, while the other is 30 miles long and 10 miles wide. Each extends to nearly 1,000ft below the water.

Such icebergs are created only rarely – there may be a decade or more between them, so two in a year is unusual. But what happened next was most surprising to scientists.

Earlier this year the two icebergs grounded on the sea bed near McMurdo Sound, an area favoured by penguins because of its rich food supplies.

The icebergs then blocked the water and wind currents that prevent ice building up. This allowed a huge sheet of ice to extend outwards into the Ross Sea and sharply decrease the fertility of the underlying water.

Researchers report that many of the penguins are taking refuge on passing icebergs – but these are too exposed and unstable for them to build nests. Emperor penguins will breed on sea ice, but only if it is stuck close to the shore. Adelie penguins will not lay eggs unless they have rocks or other material to build a nest.

The prospects for the colonies are bleak. Scientists say the icebergs could remain where they are for decades.

The colonies at Cape Crozier were the first to be discovered. Robert Falcon Scott, the Antarctic explorer, sent men to visit them at the beginning of the 20th century, before his doomed expedition to the South Pole.

A classic story of Antarctic science and adventure, *The Worst Journey in the World* by Aspley Cherry-Garrard, includes a description of an attempt by three of Scott's men to collect the first Emperor penguin eggs.

The eggs were scientific curiosities because the penguins were incorrectly believed to be a "missing link" between dinosaurs and birds. The researchers survived blizzards and were confined for several days to a makeshift shelter in their quest for the eggs.

The Adelie colony at Cape Royds also has historic links. Next to it is a hut erected by Shackleton during his first Antarctic expedition.

Adelie penguins are also in peril in other parts of Antarctica, particularly in the spit of land that projects northwards towards the tip of South America.

Almost all of the important penguin colonies on this peninsula are declining sharply. The reason is uncertain but global warming could be involved.

Scientists studying fossilised penguin remains near Britain's Antarctic research station at Rothera say far fewer Adelie penguins were there during warmer periods in the past.

Scientists working thousands of miles away at Australia's Mawson research station on the other side of the continent have reported similar declines – accelerated recently by a mystery illness that could have been brought to Antarctica by humans.

It has also been a bad year for the thousands of Emperor penguins near Britain's Halley research base. The ice broke up early, before the chicks were old enough to fend for themselves – and most of them drowned or died from hypothermia.

② Read the following advertisement, 'A surprise around every corner', as a media text, then answer the questions that follow.

Answer all three parts of the question.

a) What are the different purposes of this advertisement and what is its intended audience?

⑧

b) Examine the ways in which language is used to convey meaning in the advertisement.

⑧

c) How does the choice of form, layout and presentation contribute to the effectiveness of the advertisement?

⑨

TOTAL 25

A surprise round every corner

That's what you'll find in beautiful Dumfries & Galloway. Here in the south west corner of Scotland, where the hills are gentle and the seaside is never far away, you really will happen across some of the most inspiring things, people and places you'll ever encounter on a short break.

It's so easy to get out and about and see every corner of this very special area. But you may find it takes you quite a few visits to experience absolutely everything Dumfries & Galloway has to offer. Don't worry: most visitors find themselves falling in love with the place the moment they arrive and return again and again to discover new things to enjoy.

It's so easy to get there by train or plane or car. So come and see for yourself why we call ourselves real Scotland – real close.

Relax and find time for you

Quality time. Relaxing time. Time to call your own. A break in Dumfries & Galloway is all about making great memories for yourself. You can explore at your own pace and do just as you much – or as little – as you please. The place is such a refreshing change from the stresses and strains of everyday life and you can be sure you'll return home invigorated after even the shortest visit.

The refreshingly different break

You want busy market towns with lots of shops, museums, galleries, restaurants and friendly pubs? You want sleepy little seaside villages where the rise and fall of the tide is the only sign of time's passage? How about country walks and the chance to see some of the rarest wildlife in the British Isles?

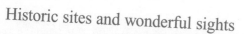

(Otters, Natterjack Toads and Golden Eagles all live here.) Fancy a round or two of golf on some of the most scenic courses in the country – and where you practically never have to queue to tee off? Dumfries & Galloway is your kind of place – and we want to welcome you here soon.

Win a break in Dumfries & Galloway absolutely free!

Here's your chance to win a short break in our fascinating corner of Scotland! When you apply for your Holiday and Short Breaks Guide (fill the coupon overleaf or call us on 08457 00 22 55) you'll be entered into a prize draw. Our lucky winner will enjoy a two night break for two at a 4 star Hotel in Dumfries & Galloway. So what are you waiting for? Pop our coupon in the post (it's completely free!) or make a quick phone call. We want to see you relaxing and enjoying some quality time here in Dumfries and Galloway soon!

Historic sites and wonderful sights

So much history has been made in Dumfries & Galloway – and the landscape is a testament to this fact. You'll find ancient castles and beautiful old abbeys here. You can visit the sites of bloody battles where the course of Scotland's history was forged. You can see the places that inspired Robert Burns to write some of his most famous poetry. And those friendly folk you meet over a beer in the local could well be ancestors of the very characters Burns wrote about!

Prize draw rules 1. Closing date for entry into the free prize draw is 31st May 2002. 2. Only one entry per household. 3. Employees of Dumfries & Galloway Tourist Board, their agencies and immediate families are not eligible to enter. 4. The winner will be notified by post by 14th June 2002. 5. The winner's name will be available after the 14th June 2002 by applying in writing enclosing a stamped, self-addressed envelope and writing to: Spring Prize Draw, Dumfries & Galloway Tourist Board, 64 Whitesands, Dumfries DH1 2RS. 6. No cash alternative will be offered. 7. All entrants must be aged 18 or over. 8. The prize is a 2 night break at a 4 star Hotel in Dumfries & Galloway. 9. Accommodation is subject to availability. 10. The promoter of this prize draw is Dumfries & Galloway Tourist Board.

Do something different. Call 08457 00 33 55

Writing on media texts

③ Study the following two advertisements 'Brains and Brawn' and 'Solar Shield'. Compare the ways in which they use various techniques in order to have an impact on the reader. You should focus on the following aspects:

- the ways in which each advertisement uses language to achieve its effects
- the layout
- the use of illustrations.

Explain which advertisement you find most effective? Give reasons for your choice. (25)

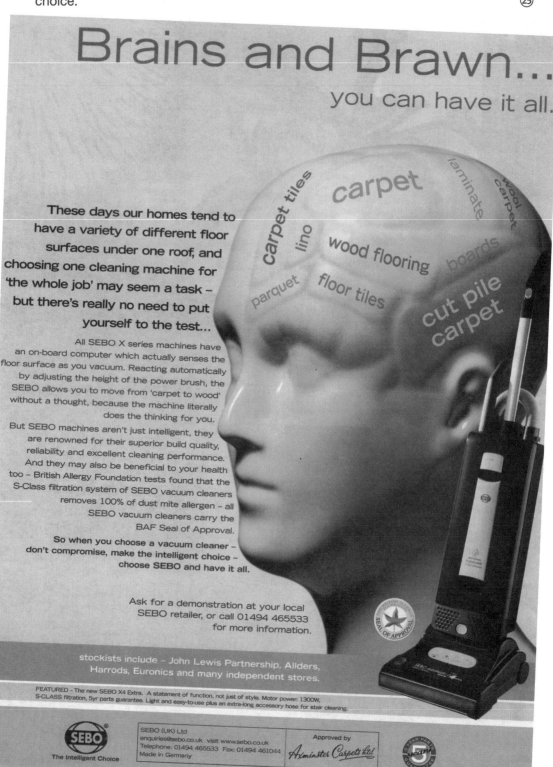

Unique wrap around design provides 40% more protection than other sunglasses.

Wear alone, with contacts or over regular glasses.

FROM ONLY £9.95 + £2.95 p&p Complete with case

Shields delicate skin around the eyes.

Virtually unbreakable lenses are hard coated to resist scratching.

Give your eyes 100% protection from harmful UV rays with SolarShield Wraparounds.

We all know that we must protect our skin if we spend lots of time in the sun. Yet apart from the use of conventional sunglasses which offer only limited protection, we tend to leave our eyes and their sensitive tissue relatively unprotected. SolarShields with their wraparound design are one of the fastest growing styles around and offer maximum UV and glare protection - **40% more than conventional sunglasses.**

Dark grey, with optical quality lenses, SolarShields are scratch and impact resistant, making them ideal for sport as well as sunbathing. With the polarised option featured above, glare from reflective surfaces such as snow or water is eliminated. **Designed to fit all sizes, you can even wear these over your ordinary glasses** saving you £££'s on prescription sunglasses.

SolarShields are laboratory tested to exceed USA, NASI and FDA standards, making them the No1 best selling protective sunglasses. Recommended by leading ophthalmologists worldwide. No wonder sales now exceed **30 million pairs.**

100% Block UVA/UVB	✓
Fits over prescription glasses	✓
Impact resistant	✓
New wrap around design	✓
Polarised option	✓

No1 PROTECTIVE SUNGLASSES Over 30 Million Sold Worldwide!

Order anytime by telephone **0800 698 7542** or by completing the coupon below. SolarShield Wraparounds comes with a 30 Day Money Back Guarantee of Satisfaction.

The Original **Solar Shield**® For Healthier Eyes

SAVE UP TO £20

Buy more than one pair for yourself or perhaps for a friend and you can **SAVE UP TO £20**

SEE ORDER FORM FOR DETAILS

Peace of Mind Guarantee

SolarShields are recommended for maximum protection by leading eye care specialists. If you are not completely satisfied, you may return them - within 30 days for an immediate - no questions asked refund.

UKHS, St George's Place, St Peter Port, GY1 2BH.

CREDIT / SWITCH CARD HOLDERS PHONE FREE ANYTIME - QUOTE UV16 **0800 698 7542** OR COMPLETE THIS COUPON

Complete and post today to: Solar Shields, Dept UV16, Freepost 3009, Oxford OX1 1YG.

	Qty. (Pairs)	Price	P&P	Total	Saving	Tick to order
Solar Shield STANDARD	1	£9.95	£2.95	£12.90		
	2	£16.95	£2.95	£19.90	Save £5.90	
	3	£22.95	£2.95	£25.90	Save £12.80	
Solar Shield POLARISED	1	£14.95	£2.95	£17.90	-	
	2	£24.95	£2.95	£27.90	Save £7.90	
	3	£29.95	£2.95	£32.90	Save £20.80	

I enclose my cheque/PO for £_____ made payable to Solar Shields. Or please debit my Master/Visa/Switch

Total Order Value £

Card No.

Expiry date /

Mr/Mrs/Miss/Ms

Address

Postcode

Signature X

Telephone

Orders are despatched within 48 hours but please allow up to 14 days for delivery. Further offers which may be of interest, may be sent to you by other carefully selected companies. If you do not want to receive them, please write to us at the above address.

Writing on media texts

EXAMINER'S TIP

General advice
These kinds of questions do not have 'right' or 'wrong' answers and very often they can be approached in many different ways. Here are some general points to bear in mind.

- *Be clear in your mind about the purpose of the writing you are examining and the audience that you think it is addressed to.*
- *Where required, make sure that you use specific details of language use to support your ideas.*
- *Be aware of features such as the use of layout, photographs, illustrations, etc. and have some ideas about how they add to the impact of the piece.*
- *Write in well-structured sentences and make sure that your spelling and punctuation are accurate.*
- *Present your work well.*

1

a)
- The use of words like 'disaster', 'huge', 'hundreds of thousands', etc. give a sense of the scale of the disaster.
- 'Trapped', 'refuge', 'perished', give a sense of the penguins' plight.
- The play on the phrase 'pick up a penguin' (a reference to the alliterative chocolate biscuit advertisement).
- Direct quotations from experts are used both to convey information and to give examples of the views held about the birds' situation.
- The reference to Shackleton and Scott give a historical perspective emphasising the fact that this colony of birds has existed a long time.
- Geographical details are given.
- Information on recent research into the penguins is given to provide background.

b)
- You should comment on how effectively the content is conveyed to the reader.
- The headline 'Penguins die in ice limbo' is emotive and has impact in terms of capturing the sympathies of the reader.
- The combination of this headline with the photograph of the penguins increases this effect.
- The accompanying maps and satellite pictures graphically show the situation, which could be difficult to convey in words alone.

- You should comment on the different experts whose views are offered and think about the purpose of including these views.

EXAMINER'S TIP

This kind of question requires both detailed analysis of language and a careful examination of all the other features of the article which contribute to its impact, such as photographs, diagrams, print size, layout, etc.

2

a)
- To promote Dumfries and Galloway as a holiday destination.
- To describe its location.
- To describe its various attractions.
- To give information about how to find out more about the area.
- To promote the area by offering a prize draw for a short-break holiday in the area.

b)
- The use of the direct address to the reader – 'you'll find…', 'you really will…', 'it takes you…' etc. creates an immediate sense of involvement and makes the reader imagine they are there.
- The use of positive language creates a favourable picture – beautiful, gentle, inspiring, quality time, etc.
- References to specific rare birds and animals are used to emphasise the special quality of the area.
- The use of persuasive language to encourage the reader to enter the prize draw.
- The use of 'we' – '…we want to welcome you', 'we want to see you', give the impression of a personalised invitation and a friendly welcome waiting for the potential visitor.

c)
- Comment on the use of the sub-headings and their effect.
- The structure of the piece which is organised to cover the different aspects of the area.
- The breaking of the text into smaller units.
- The use of photographs.
- The layout of the leaflet.

❸   Brains and Brawn

- The heading 'Brains and Brawn...you can have it all' catches the attention and gives the impression that you can have the best of all worlds.
- The text outlines the difficulty of finding one cleaner suitable for all tasks.
- Hi-tech impression given by references to 'on-board computer' etc.
- Gives the impression that the vacuum cleaner can 'think' and is actually 'intelligent'.
- The 'build quality' is stressed with terms like 'superior', 'reliability'.
- Health benefits are stressed too and reference made to the 'Seal of Approval' from the British Allergy Foundation tests and the BAF Seal of Approval is included.
- The illustration of the vacuum cleaner set against the head reinforces the idea of the 'thinking cleaner' and the head has on it all the things that the cleaner can cope with.
- The price of the cleaner is not included.

Solar Shield

- The first thing you notice is the large photograph of the glasses themselves – this dominates the visual impact of the advert.
- Key features are pointed out on the photograph.
- Next to them is the price, which seems quite cheap.
- The sub-heading, underlined for more impact, gives the vital information that the glasses give 100% protection from 'harmful UV rays'.
- The text gives information about the importance of protecting ourselves from harmful UV rays and the advantages of Solar Shields over conventional sunglasses.
- The laboratory tests of various bodies are stressed and that the glasses are 'recommended by leading opthalmologists worldwide'.
- The huge sales figures – '30 million pairs' – are also stressed.
- The checklist gives clear information of the advantages.
- This is placed next to the box 'No 1 Protective sunglasses'.
- The saving that can be made by buying more than one pair is stressed.
- An order coupon is included.
- The 'Peace of Mind Guarantee' is designed to give confidence as you can have your money back if you are not satisfied.

CHAPTER 6

Writing on non-fiction texts

To revise this topic more thoroughly, see Chapter 6 in Letts *Revise GCSE English Study Guide*.

 Try this sample GCSE question and then compare your answer with the Grade C and Grade A model answers on pages 62–64.

This question is based on *Look Forward to a Better Future*, a leaflet encouraging people to join Friends of the Earth, and the article entitled 'Putting the Life Back'. Read both through thoroughly.

Do **both** tasks.

Spend one hour on this question.

Task One

Look again at the leaflet *Look Forward to a Better Future*.

Summarise the information given in the leaflet about the work and achievements of Friends of the Earth and why they need support.

Write about 250 words in total.

Use your own words as far as possible. [10]

Task Two

Read both texts again.

Explain how each writer uses content and language to engage the interest of the reader. [15]

(Total 25 marks)

Five goods reasons to support Friends of the Earth

We are effective: our campaigners get politicians and industry to take action – through persuasive argument, lobbying and use of the law when necessary.

We are authoritative: our pioneering research is widely used by governments, commerce, the media and other environmental organisations.

We inform: we publish a broad range of information to help everyone find out about and take action on environmental problems that affect them.

We are independent: we work with all political parties, but are aligned to none.

We work at all levels: from our participation in Friends of the Earth International to the work carried out by over 250 local groups, we are uniquely placed to mobilise public opinion and campaign successfully – locally, nationally and internationally.

> **"Technical dialogue is often better from Friends of the Earth than from industry."**
> Dr David Slater, Chief Inspector,
> Her Majesty's Inspectorate of Pollution.

Our National Campaigns

Friends of the Earth was the first environmental pressure group in the UK to start campaigns for whales, endangered species and tropical rainforests, and against acid rain, ozone depletion and climate change.

Today we campaign on more issues than any other environmental group in the country.

Make your voice heard – join us in fighting for:

- better protection for wildlife and the countryside
- organic farming and safer food
- the protection of the world's forests
- better air quality
- reducing waste and over-consumption
- cleaner rivers and drinking water
- controls on dangerous chemicals, including pesticides
- less traffic and better public transport
- a halt to dangerous climate change
- safer and cleaner energy resources.

FRIENDS *of the*
earth
for the planet for people

Look forward to a better future

For millions of years, the Earth has sustained a wonderfully rich and interconnected **web of life**.

Now one single species – humankind – is putting it all at risk. The world's forests are **disappearing**…our air and water are no longer clean and pure…species are **dying out** at a terrifying rate…**toxic waste** is piling up…people everywhere **suffer** from pollution and environmental damage.

It needn't be like this. For 27 years Friends of the Earth has led the way in putting forward **positive solutions** to these and many other environmental problems.

Thanks to the support of people like you who share our conviction that the natural world and all living things should be treated with wisdom and respect, we've won some tremendous victories.

Our successes are your successes

With the support of people like you, and backed by careful research, Friends of the Earth has:

persuaded Parliament to pass five major environmental Acts that we helped draft and promote…**forced** UK aerosol makers to stop using ozone-destroying CFCs…**pressured** the Government to speed up the removal of pesticides and nitrates from drinking water using the European and High Courts…**pioneered** practical renewable energy and waste-recycling schemes…**stopped** the hunting of otters in Britain…**persuaded** the EC to ban the sale of all whale products …**stopped** plans to build an unsafe nuclear waste dump at Sellafield …**saved** wildlife reserves from development…**forced** major corporations to abandon destructive projects in tropical rainforests …**exposed** health-threatening traffic pollution levels…**uncovered** the location of thousands of secret toxic waste dumps…**persuaded** the largest DIY stores to stop selling peat from nature reserves and mahogany from tropical rainforests.

Join Friends of the Earth today and become part of this **powerful force** for environmental protection.

Become a Friend of the Earth

Our supporters are the key to every success we score for the planet and for people.

They finance almost all of our work. When you consider what we are up against – governments, powerful industrial interests and the huge resources at their disposal – you can appreciate how important this funding is and how much it achieves.

We can't allow environmental vandals to lay waste to the Earth. And with your help we'll be in a stronger position to stop them. Friends of the Earth already has a track record second to none in developing positive solutions to a huge range of problems – internationally, nationally and locally. It's a real force for change in a world that's stuck in a dangerous rut.

Join now to get our exciting and informative quarterly magazine, **Earth Matters**.

You get a practical FREE GIFT – 100 labels to help you re-use old envelopes – when you give £3.00 a month or more.

Every penny is desperately needed to fight new threats. Please help if you can.

Putting the Life Back

As more and more of the stewards of our countryside realise the value of hedgerows in landscape, wildlife and amenity terms, so too can the suburban gardener help to put back hedgerow species and the life they sustain.

Do you have a garden boundary you could plant up? Perhaps you have a *Cypress leylandii* hedge that has been mismanaged or has reached unruly proportions. There may even be legislation before too long that restricts the size of these hedges. Do yourself and your neighbours a favour – take all or part of it out and put in a traditional, varied hedgerow. If you value the privacy, keep part of it (birds like song thrushes and dunnocks often like to nest in it) or go for a hedge mix with species such as beech, holly and wild privet that keep their leaves all winter.

If your panel fencing has succumbed to wind and wet, the mixed hedgerow is the weather-proof alternative. You have the pleasure of selecting the species to plant and of watching them grow and develop, season by season, year by year.

Garden makeover

When I arrived at my new home in the autumn of 1997, the front garden was one of many challenges to be met. The estate agent spoke of this lifeless, gravel-covered carport as a virtue, but I knew that as soon as I was freed from DIY duties indoors I would convert it all back to the leafy green elegance of my neighbours' gardens. The car could sit on the roadside beyond. This was, after all, supposed to be a garden.

By early spring I was busy bagging up gravel and prising two-by-two paving slabs from cold, damp plastic sheeting beneath. There was hardcore and brick rubble to fork out, like some kind of fossilised potato crop – and a bumper one at that. With the masonry heaved aside and donated to local gardening causes and a farm track, I set about preparing the soil, impacted under years of vehicular activity. Hours of treading and crumbling followed – a strangely meditative pastime – as I massaged air and life back into the consolidated earth, and raked off blackened lumps that turned out to be stray chunks of breeze block. The lingering cement – muck, the local brickies call it – crumbled beautifully to stir like cakemix into a free-draining, friable soil on this finger of alluvium pointing east from the river Great Ouse.

Spring 1998 was a wash-out for many things, but for grass growing it was nirvana, and my bents and fescues soon bristled from the seedbed, at first a sheen of lime green, then a coat, and then a mop, ready for its first trim. I went for a seed mix to suit a thinner soil and endure rainless phases of an eastern summer. I wasn't looking for astroturf: I wanted character. This is the south-side of the house, and I hoped the loose, fine soil would

encourage delicate annual wild flowers and inhibit vigorous perennials. Magically, creeping camomile appeared, and to help it establish and spread I carefully mowed around it, and the bird's foot trefoil. Grasshoppers colonised, from who knows where. And the final seal of approval in late summer was a juvenile yellow wagtail, accompanied by a more streetwise juvenile pied wagtail, passing acquaintances blown in on a westerly, looking for insects on the sward.

The car on the roadside is increasingly obscured by the hedgerow plants I installed. I got these 'whips' from South Cambridgeshire District Council's nursery, a mix of thorns and field maple, with some hazel, dogwood, dogrose and wild privet. I was delighted to find an old hawthorn stump refusing to submit and sending up fresh stems, and traces of blackthorn too, when I removed some stray cypresses. The immaculately maintained elm

hedge next door also sent a sucker under the path that separates our two gardens, to add to the diversity and help make the link between our two hedgerows.

I added some cistus plants, for a Mediterranean 'maquis' feel, for scents in the summer sun, and for year-round green and drought-tolerance. I also decorated the hedgebottom with primroses, and slipped a few snowdrop and bluebell bulbs between gaps in the plastic, disguised with some left over gravel.

Elsewhere, the garden path has been lined with lavenders, broom and box. A cutting of gorse rooted well, added in the corner, where I should be able to see the sunlight radiating from its golden flowers. And nearby I squeezed in a plump foxglove, fattened and ready to produce a flowering spike the following spring. Foxgloves with gorse will remind me of Dumyat, the hill that glows as the summer sun sets over Stirling.

TOP TIPS FOR HEDGE PLANTING

- Go for a rich diversity with a solid thorn theme running through it – hawthorn and blackthorn laced with holly, guelder rose, dogrose, spindle, field maple, wild privet, dogwood and beech, for example.
- Plant in winter.
- Put plants in at 45 degrees, to encourage denser growth.
- Plant in two rows, if you can, spacing plants about 18 inches apart in each direction.
- Reduce unwanted competition by using a recycled mulch, such as old plastic sacks.
- Don't water, except in the first year or two during drought.
- Prune hard each winter, down to a strong shoot, to promote thick growth and prevent gaps low down.
- When established, trim the hedge on alternate sides each year, but not when it is flowering or fruiting; taper the sides into an A-shape to let light reach the bottom.

These two answers are at grades C and A. Compare which one your answer is closest to and think how you could have improved it.

Writing on non-fiction texts

GRADE C ANSWER

David

Task one

Clear focus on question to open.

'Friends of the Earth' basically do everything they can to protect the natural environment and the interest of many different species of animals. They persuade Parliament to pass laws against such things as the use of CFCs and to remove nitrates and pesticides from drinking water. ✓ They have also been known to use the European and High Courts to achieve their aims.

Covers a range of points.

Good summary of ideas.

'Friends of the Earth' have fought major corporations and companies for what they believe in. They have prevented the development of an 'unsafe nuclear dump at Sellafield' and prevented development from taking place on nature reserves. They not only protect the environment but protect animals too. They have persuaded the EU to ban the sale of whale products and have made the hunting of otters in Britain illegal. ✓

Explains why they need support.

'Friends of the Earth' need support because without these supporters they would not have the funds needed to carry out their work. Considering who they work against and challenge, organisations such as governments and industrial corporations who have a huge range of resources at their disposal, they need all the support that they can get. ✓   **7/10**

Task Two

Some development of ideas and examples to support points would be useful here.

The two texts studied both use very different content and language to engage the interest of the reader. The Friends of the Earth leaflet uses very persuasive and almost aggressive language and also lists fact after fact in order to maintain interest.

An example is needed here.

However, the article entitled 'Putting the Life Back' is written in a very different way. The author of this article writes the article almost like a story and uses little or no hard facts, unlike the author of the first article. The author of this article uses a few similes to help maintain a degree of interest from the reader. The reader is also shown how easily things can be changed from one thing to another and so finds inspiration from the article which may well hold their interest and encourage them to read farther. ✓

General comment – could be more specific.

Tends to repeat the point.

The author of the first article uses fact and persuasive writing to create powerful and emotive language to hold interest. The fact that the reader learns of what can be done from their very own funding also helps to maintain their interest.

Lacks specific examples of language use.

Overall these two articles are very different in the way in which they are written and presented and have different effects on the reader. Both are equally effective at engaging the interest of the reader but for very different reasons. The first article achieves this by using emotive language and the facts while the second uses everyday language in which the reader can relate to in order to hold their attention. ✓   **9/15**

Total 16/25

Grade booster ····} move C to B

Specific examples of language use and the effects created are needed here.

Fluent opening.

Good summary of function.

Sums up the key ideas effectively.

Andrew

Task One

The Friends of the Earth is an environmental pressure group. They are based in the UK but also take part in action by Friends of the Earth international. Work that is undertaken by the group is to lobby governments, local authorities and industry rather than just putting up with it. ✓

A lot of the work that the group do is to inform, as by informing people of what is going on in the environment and how it effects them, you can get them to change. The Friends of the Earth have become a leading figure in pioneering environmental research and they use this information for the good of the environment. ✓ Putting pressure on organisations to protect the environment is not an easy job. It can be done via a number of different ways like the law or by starting protests. Both of these methods take time and money, and they are why the Friends of the Earth need support. Fund raising and donations are how the group finances saving the environment. When it comes to being heard many voices are heard better than just a few and that is why the group needs to be supported. ✓   8/10

Effective opening.

Give examples of language use and effects.

Task Two

These two texts are both about the same subject, the environment. ✓ The first text 'Look Forward to a better Future' uses language in a very bold and informative manner. It lists its information in bullet points so that the reader can imediately understand what it is that they are being told without having to spend a lot time reading. ✓ This is reflected in the fact that this is a leaflet and not an article. Nor does its content go into any great detail about what the leaflet is telling you. What we get after reading this leaflet is a brief understanding of what the Friends of the Earth does and why it encourages us to go out and want to discover more on this

Example and comment on effects.

Contrast of format and comment on structure.

Develops ideas on structure and format – good analysis here.

subject. At the end it uses a quote from Her Majesty's Inspectorate of Pollution. It appears the leaflet try and uses this quote at the very end to endorse everything that has been said preveously. ✓

The second text 'Putting the Life Back' uses a completely different format to that of the first; to try and get its message across. It starts off by drawing you into the article by asking a number of questions relative to subject. The writer then goes on to make a couple of brief suggestions. This use of language is aimed at developing the readers interest in the article before the main part begins. ✓ The second part of this article is a story following the writers own experience. The writer trys to tell of what he managed to achieve, so as to say 'look if I can do this. Whats stopping you from doing it.'

Within this little story the writer gives a few little brief tips on how to go about putting in a hedgerow but only a few. This is so as not to overwelm the reader with facts while still trying to be encouraging about the subject. At the end of the article there is a Top Tips for Hedge planting box containing bullet points. Now if the article has managed to succeed in getting the reader to want to get involved in the subject, the writer has given him the tools to do so. ✓

Both texts use language and content in different ways though they end up with the same result – that of successfully getting a message across. ✓   13/15

Total 21/25

Grade booster ·····⟩ move A to A*
- Sentence structure needs attention in places – some of the phrasing is a little clumsy.
- Basic spelling errors should be avoided.

1   Spend about one hour on the following question.
Write about 300–400 words.
Leave enough time to read through and correct what you have written.

The following extract is from *An Evil Cradling* in which the writer, Brian Keenan, describes his experience of being kidnapped and held hostage by terrorists in Beirut. Here he describes the early stages of his captivity.
Read the extract through carefully and then answer the following questions.

a) What effect do you think Keenan wants to create in the mind of the reader through his writing?   ⑩

b) How does Keenan use language here to create his effects? You should focus on specific details of the ways in which he uses language in your answer.   ⑮

TOTAL 25

An Evil Cradling

My first hours, then days and then weeks I found myself constantly having to deal with the slow hallucination into which I had been dropped. I had been removed from a known reality. The four concrete walls of my shoe-box-sized cell formed my only vista. Beyond these I could see nothing, only my imagination gave me images, some beautiful, some disturbing and unendurably ever-present. The vast landscape of the mind unfolds on its own. At times I felt the compensations of this gift and at other times cursed my imagination that it could bring me sensations so contorted, so strange and so incoherent that I screamed; not out of fear but out of the rage and frustration of having to deal with these flashing pictures of which I could make little or no sense.

Exaggerating this distorted sensitivity were the voices of the captors in a disembodied language which I didn't understand but could hear being spoken, being whispered, being shouted beyond the walls of my cell. There were the cries, too, of the other prisoners, all in Arabic as I recall, some of them weeping and in the long hours of darkness some of that weeping becoming screaming. At other times the shouts came from a street vendor selling fruit or fish, reminding me starkly that there was something outside, but that I was buried away from normal life and could only hear its echo. So many thoughts, so many ideas, so many feelings came hurtling into my mind in those first days; too many to take hold of and deal with in an ordered and coherent way. You simply had to sit in lethargy, letting them wash over you and holding on to some point of resistance that would only let them wash over but not sweep you away. The dangers of that were too great and too apparent. There was nowhere to run to.

I chose, as all men in those circumstances would, to disbelieve that I would be held for very long. I immediately set a date in my head and I look back now with some amusement on it. I decided within those first few hours that I would be kept no longer than a few weeks. My nationality was worthless to them. It would be pointless to hold an Irishman: they could trade me for little or nothing. It was while thinking this through that I fixed my mind on the only option open to me: somehow to convince these men of the fruitlessness of keeping me as a hostage against some political demand. While I was forcing this belief on myself so as to hold back all the vast confusion and fear, the cell door opened for the third time on the first day.

I was given a bottle of Coke and two sandwiches wrapped in Arabic bread. I was told by the guard 'Soon, my boss he come.' I shrugged my shoulders, confident and nonchalant. The door closed again but it was not locked. I could dimly see the guards moving past. There seemed to be several of them. They hovered about my door trying to look in, me looking out, convinced that it was only in this eye contact that I could maintain a distance from them. In those first weeks when confronted by them I would not take my eyes from their faces. In the few times that I did see a face, all the faces were as one to me, each blending in to one another, and I could hardly distinguish their separate features.

The door opened again, four men in their mid-twenties, some with hand guns, peered in at me. They stood in silence. Two of them just inside the door, two of them standing in the hallway beyond, looking intently at me as I looked back at them. I felt like a fish in an aquarium. They were silent and staring and I stared back. There was something between us. Maybe it was the fear in the air.

The long minutes of gazing down at me as I sat on the floor were oppressive. Then suddenly there was movement. The men parted, and an older man in a brown suit, with grey wavy hair and a full grey beard was standing in the doorway, studying me. He was obviously a man of some rank. The other men stood back in fearful respect. He looked at me, and I looked back at him. I was unmoved and did not blink. He asked me 'Are you English?' I noted that his English was an educated one. He spoke it well and I answered him. 'No, I am not English…I am Irish.'

He looked at me again in silence, with long pauses between his questions: 'Where do you come from?' I answered with the same nonchalance, perhaps this time filled with the native stubbornness of my city: 'I'm from Belfast…Do you know it?' There was a touch of anger and aggression in my voice. He noted it, nodded, yes he knew it. He asked me how long I had been in Lebanon. I was uncomfortable that I had to sit on the floor while I was being questioned. It put me at a disadvantage. I wanted to stand up to him face to face, but something told me that it would be foolish, perhaps dangerous.

He muttered something to the guards, and there was an exchange between them. He looked back at me and asked calmly did I have an Irish passport. I told him of course I had an Irish passport. He asked 'Where is it?' I saw that it was time for a joke. 'Well if you'd like to take me back to my apartment I'll get it for you.' I smiled. He did not return the smile, but turned again to the men with the guns and said something in Arabic. There seemed to be some confusion. It was hard to tell with these excitable men. He turned and quietly told me that if I co-operated I would not be harmed. He told me he would return, and the door banged shut again. The padlock rattled, accompanied by the babble of this fearfully incomprehensible language.

from An Evil Cradling *by Brian Keenan*

(2) This question is based on the article 'Vicious Circles'.

Do both tasks.

Spend about 45 minutes on this question.

Task One

Read the article carefully.

Summarise the information you are given about Roman amphitheatres in the article.

(10)

Write about 250 words in total.

Use your own words as far as possible.

Task Two

Explore the ways in which the writer uses language to engage the interest of the reader.

(15)

TOTAL 25

Guy de la Bédoyère explains how English Heritage is gaining greater insight into Britain's Roman amphitheatres and what went on within them other than popularly imagined scenes of carnage

Vicious circles

THE HIT movie Gladiator was followed hotfoot in 2001 by some major developments in the study of Britain's Roman amphitheatres. In association with archaeological units and universities, English Heritage is applying up-to-date scientific techniques to newly discovered arenas.

A depression in a field near the Roman fort at Richborough, Kent, was known to be an amphitheatre following excavations in the nineteenth century, though its shape, size and plan had been misunderstood. Until, that is, the initiation of a project by English Heritage's Centre for Archaeology. The first stage involved a geophysical survey by the centre's archaeometry team. Deep-probing radar resistivity and mashetometer surveys have revealed the amphitheatre's full, complex shape, including a number of unsuspected details. English heritage's chief archaeologist, David Miles, is especially keen on the methods: 'They give information and fine detail of what is there on a very large scale; excavations can be far more targeted.'

The investigation also revealed the true complexity of the site as a whole, in particular the Roman town stretching from the fort to the amphitheatre, possibly a relatively late addition to the settlement.

The Richborough survey means that the English Heritage archaeological team, led by Tony Wilmott in collaboration with the universities of Kent and Southampton, Kent County Council and Professor Martin Millett of Cambridge University, is far better informed about the nature and extent of the site than were the archaeologists who excavated the Roman fort 80 years ago. It is hoped that there will be a chance to explore two anomalies on the amphitheatre plan. They might be shrines, elaborate architectural features, or even structures built much later.

The amphitheatre is the quint-essential cliché of the Roman world – to us at any rate. Their vicious fights to the death involved gladiators and often wild animals from exotic provinces such as Africa. It was Emperor Vespasian (ruled AD 69-79) who built the Colosseum, Rome's first permanent arena. He had a keen sense for entertaining the rabble. It's perhaps no coincidence that many of Roman Britain's amphitheatres were founded during his reign or those of his sons, Titus (AD 79-81) and Domitian (AD 81-96).

Educated Romans were appalled or enthralled. Pliny the Younger thought the mob's fanatical adherence to favourite fighters absurdly juvenile. The philosopher Seneca, trying to enjoy a lunchtime show, was frustrated by the perfunctory way that men were killed to clock up the numbers. 'Just plain murder,' he moaned.

When the crowd grew bored, imperial impresarios would resort to ever more extravagant blood baths. Notoriously, in AD 59 a riot exploded at the amphitheatre in Pompeii when visitors from nearby Nuceria got into a fight with locals. Outnumbered, many Nucerians were killed. The Senate were so disgusted that it closed the arena for 10 years.

Blood and gore aside, amphitheatres had a more sophisticated role to play. The Roman world was the ultimate multi-ethnic melting pot. Roman Britain had soldiers, officials and traders from Gaul, Germany and as far away as North Africa and Syria, as well as Britons who adopted Roman ways. Reinforcing the Roman tie that held them together was vital.

The Roman army's amphitheatres were probably used for military drills, but also for unifying displays of martial skill, similar to the way that dogfights between restored Spitfires and cod Messerschmitts at military air shows help commemorate modern history. Soldiers gathered there, too, to

ANSWERS ON PAGE 72 ANSWERS ON PAGE 72 ANSWERS ON PAGE 72 ANSWERS ON PAGE 72

worship their emperor and to watch staged mythical battles.

Perhaps London's recently discovered amphitheatre played host to such spectacles, though it may also have been used for public executions. It lies within the Roman city walls but close to London's Roman fort – home to the governor's garrison, made up of detachments taken from the Roman legions stationed at York, Chester and Caerleon.

Romano-British amphitheatres were not built of arches and vaults like the Colosseum (and none had the plumbing facilities for putting on mock sea battles). Excavations for English Heritage at Silchester in Hampshire, once a Roman regional capital, have shown that the arena was cut into the ground, with the dug-out soil then used to build earthen banks. These supported rows of wooden seats with room for thousands.

One of Britain's biggest, Chester's amphitheatre belonged to the city's huge legionary fortress – housing some 5,500 soldiers, their families and slaves, traders and other hangers-on. Originally a small scale timber arena, it was later rebuilt in stone on a grander scale, probably by the XX Legion whose home this was for at least 200

Above: aerial view of the Frilford site

Previous page and above: the amphitheatre at Silchester which could accommodate thousands

years. Clues about what went on there come from the shrine to Nemesis beside the arena – a centurion called Sextus Marcianus dedicated an altar to the goddess of fate – and a carved relief found nearby depicting a retiarius, a gladiator armed with a net and a trident.

The site was partly excavated in the 1960s. In the mid-1980s, plans were drawn up to excavate the rest, but the money never materialised. The Grade II listed eighteenth-century Dee House, the County Court and car park on the site currently prevent further excavation.

Chester's amphitheatre is now the focus of heated local debate. Some want to see it made into a full-scale heritage attraction, while others see preserving Dee House as more important. So a conservation plan has been commissioned to look into the significance of the different phases of the site's development from the pre-Roman period to the present day. Little is known of the city's post-Roman archaeology or the amphitheatre's origins and this might be the place to find out more. Trial re-excavation in the exposed half of the amphitheatre in 2000 and 2001 suggests that significant archaeological evidence remains to be explored, the 1960s excavations notwithstanding.

Henry Owen-John, English Heritage's assistant director for the North-West, hopes that Chester's amphitheatre will become a more prominent and informative place to visit. 'I'd like to see significant additional research excavation leading to exposure at least of the amphitheatre's western entrance, to make the site more intelligible,' he says. One intriguing possibility is the use of a geological survey. The buried half might well give up some of its secrets this way and Henry believes this information is needed to make decisions about whether the site should be excavated more extensively.

The civilians of Roman Britain were certainly familiar with amphitheatres, a handy indication of civic prestige. At Cirencester in Gloucestershire, once the second largest city in Roman Britain, an old stone quarry was transformed into an arena. At Dorchester, Dorset, a Neolithic henge monument dating around 2000BC was similarly converted. Aerial photographs and a geophysical survey show another amphitheatre south of the walls at the small Roman regional capital of Caistor-by-Norwich.

Like the military versions, civilian amphitheatres may have featured

HERITAGE TODAY

Left and above: the remains of the amphitheatre at Silchester show how it was cut into the ground and built

culture as well as, or instead of, carnage. Theatres and amphitheatres were sometimes built close to temples and so far none of Britain's amphitheatres has produced a trace of gladiatorial equipment.

More aerial photography has found an amphitheatre at Frilford, Oxford-shire: a large temple site straddling an ancient tribal boundary. Remarkably, the name of the field where it was found, Trendles, provides a clue, it comes from the Old English 'trendel', meaning circle or disc.

Frilford is currently the focus of a long-term training project run by Oxford's Institute of Archaeology. As at Richborough, work began with geo-physics, which also revealed a large and enigmatic building beside the amphitheatre itself – and possible evi-dence of an Iron-Age religious settlement, too.

The prospects are exciting. We're likely to find out a good deal more about what went on in Romano-British amphitheatres, and how they were used in a broad range of different settlements. But these long-term projects are also paths into the archaeological future. Site manage-ment will be based on increasingly comprehensive information, while excavation work, as David Miles points out, can be 'like brain surgery rather than an autopsy'.

FACT FILE

Chester, Roman Deva (Cheshire). Map ref: SJ 405658. Open any reasonable time. Half the arena, two entrances, earthern banks, and shrine.

Cirencester, Roman Corinium Dobunnorum (Gloucestershire). Map ref: SP 020014. Open any reasonable time. Earthern banks and arena.

Silchester, Roman Calleva Atrebatum (Hampshire). Map ref: SU 643624. Open any reasonable time. Arena, banks, stone revetments and shrine.

Other impressive remains can be seen at Maumbury Rings, just south of modern Dorchester, Dorset, and in Gwent at Caerleon.

HERITAGE TODAY

Writing on non-fiction texts

3 The following article is about how the lives of the people living on the tiny island of Montserrat in the West Indies were instantly disrupted when its mountain volcano erupted in June 1997 for the second time in less than two years.

Read it through carefully and answer the following questions.

a) Explain what you have learnt from the article about the impact of volcanic eruptions on Montserrat and the people who live there. (10)

b) What do you think are the writer's implied opinions about the problems facing small island communities and how have these views been expressed effectively? (15)

TOTAL 25

The people of Montserrat were still coping with the consequences of events in December 1995, when the volcano erupted for the first time after lying dormant for four centuries. This earlier eruption reduced the island's population of 11,000 to under 7,000 as many people left for neighbouring countries. Many of the remaining islanders have been living away from their homes for the last two years, living in military-style tents – with no gas or electricity – and a row of pit toilets outside. Conditions are unsanitary and overcrowded.

The natural environment and topography of the island has also suffered long-term damage, as sulphurous gases were released into the atmosphere and began to form acid rain. It burned the mountaintop vegetation and increased the acidity of lakes and streams, to such an extent that marine life such as fish and plankton could not survive. These natural resources were vital to the islanders, many of whom earn their living by farming and fishing.

Need to evacuate

After the recent eruption, islanders were advised to shelter under strong roofs and wear protective headgear because of falling rocks and ash. Masks had to be worn outdoors to protect them from the hazardous fumes. This continuous eruption has laid most of the southern side of the island to waste, with farmland and crops buried under tons of hot ash. Scientists predict it could take months for land surfaces to cool. The islanders were told to prepare to evacuate and pack extra food, water, medicine and personal items. They were given the option of relocating to Britain or another island, or remaining on the northern side of Montserrat which is now thought to have good potential for development.

The impact of a volcano on such a small island is long lasting and totally devastating - not just to the local people and the environment - but to the economy and long-term development. The Montserrat government had to set up a basic infrastructure to cope with the disaster - additional water resources within the safe zone, shelter with cooking facilities to cater for children and the old and infirm, and an emergency transport service to cover the island. Those who stayed are trying to fend for themselves; some have re-planted gardens with vegetables; a primary school has been restarted with 50 pupils attending.

The UK connection

The Island's government called for emergency relief from the UK in particular because of its historical relationship as a 'Dependent Territory', and became embroiled in a controversy with the British Labour government, much of which is now being resolved. Support has been pledged for a five-year plan to rebuild Montserrat, to construct a new capital and 250 homes in the northern safe zone. According to the Department for International Development here in the UK, each resident has been offered £3,500 to temporarily relocate to a neighbouring country, or two-year citizenship to stay in this country, with their future status uncertain. But most Montserratians insist that no amount of money could compensate for the lives and homes that have been destroyed. They want a secure and sustainable future on their island home.

There are several Montserrat community groups in the UK who are bringing attention to their cause and raising money to support the plight of their fellow Montserratians.

Small islands

For most of us, small islands conjure up images of paradise on earth. But for the inhabitants of these islands, life is often a struggle for survival, made more difficult being small and marginalised by the rest of the world. In recent years, the threats to their way of life have increased and intensified.

Small islands are particularly vulnerable and are widely seen as being in the front-line of the impact of climate change, such as rising sea levels, (which could totally submerge some of the low-lying islands) and violent storms. Whether it is a volcano or rising sea levels, in some cases, whole nations may have to be resettled. No-one knows yet what will happen to them. They are also at risk from industrial exploitation like toxic waste dumping, and the negative impacts of tourism and economic dependence.

Most small islands suffer from a balance of payments problem. They need so many goods that they cannot manufacture themselves that they cannot export enough to pay for them all. In the short term at least, support from countries of the North in the form of financial and technical help is essential. But in the longer term many island governments are seeking sustainable ways of developing and making themselves more economically independent.

Despite these unique challenges, the governments of small island developing states around the world are beginning to organise themselves together and fight for their special interests. There are 41 member states of the Alliance of Small Island States (AOSIS). They have rich marine resources that make them crucial contributors to the world's protein supply.

4 The following article is taken from the RSPCA's web page and concerns the suffering often caused to wild reptiles kept in captivity. Read it through carefully and then answer the following questions.

a) What do you learn about the plight of many reptiles kept in captivity? ⑩

b) How are the writer's views on this subject revealed to the reader? You should use specific details from the text to support your ideas. ⑮

TOTAL 25

News – Reptiles are dying of starvation

Thousands of vulnerable wild-caught reptiles are dying from bone disease and severe digestive disorders like anorexia, a shocking new RSPCA report has revealed.

The Society is hoping these new findings will force the EU to act and is calling for the import of the most vulnerable species such as chameleons, some snakes, crocodilians and certain species of lizard, into the EU to be banned.

Reptiles need highly specialized diets but evidence shows that some ignorant owners feed their vegetarian pets on cat and dog food. In other instances, reptiles were kept in climatic conditions that can cause food to rot in the animal's intestine, according to the report *Far from home*.

Welfare problems

All those species singled out by the RSPCA as vulnerable can grow to be large, dangerous, highly active or need extremely specialist care. By analysing trade related publications the report highlights the variety of welfare problems involved in keeping reptiles and lists the causes of sickness and death experienced during transportation and while reptiles are kept in captivity.

Far from home reveals that malnutrition is found in about 15 per cent of pet reptiles and highlights a range of other health problems including rickets, osteoporosis, respiratory diseases and serious skin loss that can cause the reptile to die. The report also shows that pet reptiles are often not provided with the right lighting and temperature levels reflecting seasonal patterns, some suffer serious burns from incorrectly fitted heaters and many enclosures are too small.

As the EU has imported millions of live reptiles and is one of the world's main markets, the RSPCA believes it should ban or further restrict the trade in certain species but has failed to do so. The Society hopes the new report showing the high death and sickness rate of captive reptiles will now push the EU to introduce new measures to enforce existing legislation.

Specialized diets

RSPCA chief veterinary officer Chris Laurence said: 'The current system is failing to protect many reptiles. A ban on the trade of those species identified as the most vulnerable is the only way to prevent suffering. Individual reptiles need highly specialized diets. But there is evidence that some are badly kept leading to such problems as bone disease, pneumonia and mouth rot.'

While the RSPCA believes exotics such as reptiles do not make suitable pets, it wants to ensure that those who are determined to own reptiles are adequately informed about the needs of the animal – a measure which the government has failed to implement through EU legislation for the last five years.

Writing on non-fiction texts

Writing on non-fiction texts

EXAMINER'S TIP

General advice
These kinds of questions do not have 'right' or
'wrong' answers and very often they can be
approached in many different ways. Here are
some general points to bear in mind:
- *Be clear in your mind about the purpose of*
  the writing you are examining and the
  audience that you think it is addressed to.
- *Where required make sure that you use*
  specific details of language use to support
  your ideas.
- *Write in well-structured sentences and*
  make sure that your spelling and
  punctuation are accurate.
- *Present your work well.*

①

a)
- Keenan wants to give the reader a vivid
  impression of the experience of being held
  captive.
- He conveys an impression of his state of
  mind and wants to share this with his
  reader.
- He also gives details of his captors and the
  way they treated him.

b)
- In the first paragraph Keenan expresses
  how the whole experience seemed unreal –
  note his use of words and phrases such as
  'hallucination' and 'removed from reality'.
  The sense of his mind finding it difficult to
  comprehend what is happening to him is
  brought out here.
- In the second paragraph the emphasis is
  very much on the sounds that Keenan can
  hear from his 'shoe-box-sized cell'. This is
  not surprising as he can see little from this
  tiny prison – note the references to the
  voices of his captors speaking Arabic
  (increasing his sense of alienation and fear),
  the screaming and weeping in the darkness,
  etc.
- In the third paragraph he tries to force his
  mind to come to terms with his situation
  and he reveals the thoughts that are
  running through his head – note references
  to 'head', 'thinking', 'forcing this belief',
  'vast confusion and fear' create an
  impression of his state of mind here.
- Paragraphs four and five develop the
  relationship between Keenan and his
  guards – notice the references to 'eye
  contact' and the frequent references to
  'looking', 'staring', etc.

- In paragraphs six, seven and eight a new
  character is introduced – the 'man of some
  rank' – and Keenan gives details of his
  questioning. Notice his use of direct speech
  here through which he helps to re-create
  the experience for his reader.

EXAMINER'S TIP

Make sure that you focus closely on the ways
in which language is used to create a sense of
the experience and to re-create the
atmosphere and state of mind of the writer.
Use specific examples to illustrate your ideas.

② **Task One**
- Up-to-date archaeological techniques are
  being used to investigate newly discovered
  arenas.
- English amphitheatres are discussed.
- The bloody use to which they were put is
  discussed.
- Other, less known uses, are discussed.
- Specific sites are examined.
- The article points to the exciting prospect of
  finding out more about what went on in
  Romano-British amphitheatres.

Task Two
- The article begins with a reference to the
  film *Gladiator* which immediately captures
  the reader's attention.
- Some 'scientific' language is used to
  describe the excavations, e.g. 'geophysical',
  'resistivity' etc.
- The article uses historical references and
  dates to help put the information in
  context.
- The article combines quite complex
  language with straightforward such as
  'Seneca, trying to enjoy a lunchtime show'
  and 'men were killed to clock up the
  numbers'.
- The article tries to bring the pictures to life
  for the reader by describing activities that
  may have taken place.
- Several modern archaeologists are
  mentioned and their work described.

a)
- The population of the island have been significantly reduced.
- The islanders remaining have had to live away from their homes for the last two years.
- Their living conditions are poor – they are overcrowded and unsanitary.
- The natural environment has been severely damaged.
- Farming and fishing, vital to the economy and survival of the islanders have been devastated.

b)
- The description of the poor living conditions of the islander reveals sympathy for their plight.
- The description of those who stayed on the island 'trying to fend for themselves' and the images of them replanting and starting up the school again also create a feeling of sympathy.
- The tone seems to be one of admiration for the islanders' steadfastness and resilience to come back from the devastation that the eruption had brought to their lives.
- The reference to the controversy over emergency relief and the idea that no money could compensate them for what they have lost again create a sense of sympathy.
- The contrast between the popular image of the idyllic nature of life on a small island with the harsh reality of the struggle for survival that often occurs suggests that the writer appreciates how tough life can often be for such islanders.
- This is reinforced by the list of threats facing the inhabitants of small islands.

a)
- Thousands of wild-caught reptiles are dying of bone disease and digestive disorders.
- They are not being fed the specialised diet they need.
- The report *Far from home* has revealed that malnutrition is found in about 15 per cent of pet reptiles.
- The report has also highlighted a range of other problems that cause sickness and death to these reptiles such as bone diseases and respiratory diseases.
- Many are not provided with the appropriate lighting and temperature levels.
- Many are kept in enclosures that are too small.

b)
- The reference to the new RSPCA report as 'shocking' immediately reveals the writer's attitude.
- The Society is 'hoping' that the findings will 'force' the EU to take action.
- The reference to 'ignorant owners'.
- The list of things that these reptiles suffer.
- The fact the EU has failed to act to ban the huge number of imports of live reptile ('millions').
- The fact that the EU has not enforced existing legislation.
- The use of the quotation from the RSPCA's chief veterinary officer talking of the 'suffering' caused.
- The reference to the government's 'failure' to implement measures through EU legislation.

Writing on non-fiction texts

CHAPTER 7

Writing on literary texts

To revise this topic more thoroughly, see Chapter 10 in Letts *Revise GCSE English Study Guide*.

 Try this sample GCSE question and then compare your answer with the Grade C and Grade A model answers on pages 76–79.

Look at the poems 'Leaving School' and 'Dear Mr Lee'.

Compare the ways in which the two poets present experiences of school, and the thoughts and the feelings of the narrator of each poem.

In your answer you should consider closely the poets' use of language.

(25 marks)

Leaving School

I was eight when I set out into the world
wearing a grey flannel suit.
I had my own suitcase.
I thought it was going to be fun.
I wasn't listening
when everything was explained to us in the Library,
so the first night I didn't have any sheets.
The headmaster's wife told me
to think of the timetable as a game of 'Battleships'.
She found me walking around upstairs
wearing the wrong shoes.

I liked all the waiting we had to do at school
but I didn't like the work.
I could only read certain things
which I'd read before, like the Billy Goat Gruff books,
but they didn't have them here.
They had the Beacon Series.
I said 'I don't know,'
then I started saying nothing.
Every day my name was read out
because I'd forgotten to hang something up.

I was so far away from home I used to forget things.
I forgot how to get undressed.
You're supposed to take off your shirt and vest
after you've put on your pyjama bottoms.

When the headmaster's wife came round for Inspection
I was fully dressed again, ready for bed.
She had my toothbrush in her hand
and she wanted to know why it was dry.
I was miles away, with my suitcase, leaving school.

Hugo Williams

Dear Mr Lee

Dear Mr Lee (Mr Smart says
It's rude to call you Laurie, but that's
How I think of you, having lived with you
Really all year). Dear Mr Lee
(Laurie) I just want you to know
I used to hate English, and Mr Smart
Is roughly my least favourite person,
And as for Shakespeare (we're doing him too)
I think he's a national disaster, with all those jokes
That Mr Smart has to explain why they're jokes
And even then no one thinks they're funny,
And T. Hughes and P. Larkin and that lot
In our anthology, not exactly a laugh a minute,
Pretty gloomy really, so that's why
I wanted to say Dear Laurie (sorry) your book's
The one that made up for the others, if you
Could see my copy you'd know it's lived
With me, stained with Coke and Kitkat
And when I had a cold, and I often
take you to bed with me to cheer me up
So Dear Laurie, I want to say sorry,
I didn't want to write a character-sketch
Of your mother under headings, it seemed
Wrong somehow when you'd made her so lovely,
And I didn't much like those questions
About *social welfare in the rural community*
And *the seasons as perceived by an adolescent*,
I didn't think you'd want your book
Read that way, but bits of it I know by heart,
And I wish I had your uncles and your half-sister
And lived in Slad, though Mr Smart says your view
Of the class struggle is naïve, and the examiners
Won't be impressed by me knowing so much by heart,
They'll be looking for terse and cogent answers
To their questions, but I'm not much good at terse and cogent,
I'd just like to be like you, not mind about being poor,
See everything bright and strange, the way you do,
And I've got the next one out of the Public Library,
About Spain, and I asked Mum about learning
To play the fiddle, but Mr Smart says Spain isn't
Like that anymore, it's all Timeshare villas
And Torremolinos, and how old were you
When you became a poet? (Mr Smart says for anyone
With my punctuation to consider poetry as a career
Is enough to make the angels weep).

PS Dear Laurie, please don't feel guilty
For me failing the exam, it wasn't your
Fault, it was mine, and Shakespeare's,
And maybe Mr Smart's, I still love *Cider*,
It hasn't made any difference.

U. A. Fanthorpe

These two answers are at grades C and A. Compare which one your answer
is closest to and think how you could have improved it.

GRADE C ANSWER

*A very general introduction that
doesn't really say much.*

*Not well expressed – trying to
analyse but not putting across
the point clearly.*

Again not clearly expressed.

A good point here.

Some relevant analysis.

*Makes connection between
poems here.*

Tony

These two poets have written two contrasting poems about
their memories of school life. The first one is called 'Leaving
School' and is by a poet called Hugo Williams. Whilst the
second by U.A. Fanthorpe is call 'Dear Mr Lee'. These two
poems have both their similarities and differences in the way
that they have been written. ✓

Leaving School has been split into three equally sized verses,
this gives the idea that the poem has been well structed and
layed out. How in comparison Dear Mr Lee is just one long
verse, and gives the good impression of a child spilling out
words. Neither of these two styles of poetry is bad or wrong
they just both portray the narrator's feelings well. Another
difference between the two poems is the amount of and use
of characters. ✓ Leaving School has two characters, though
after reading it I feel that there really is only the one. This is
because of lines like 'The headmaster's wife told me'.

This gives me the feeling that the young boy, that the
poem is based on, see's her as just an object that tells
him what to do not as a person. It can also be seen like
this because she is reffered to as 'the headmaster's wife'
and not by name.

Dear Mr Lee is centred around three characters. The boy
who is narrating the poem, his teacher Mr Smart and the
poet Laurie Lee. Unlike as with Leaving School these characters
add depth to poem and are a large part of it. After reading
it out loud a few times the poem has some rythem to it
with lines like 'Dear Laurie (sorry)' helping it to roll off the
tongue well because it rymes. ✓

Both poems make good use of personal pronouns this gives
the narrator a strong sense of character, gives the poems
personal status and shows that the narrator is speaking directly
to the audience. Leaving School makes especially good use of
personal pronouns with large use of 'I'. This backs up my
earlier theory of it only being centred on one character, the
narrator. Also with Leaving School I feel that the narrator
didn't enjoy boarding school and didn't want to be there,
but would rather be off doing his own thing. Perhaps back at
home with his old friends. On the other hand the narrator in
Dear Mr Lee has come to enjoy a subject at school he didn't
like before reading the book by Mr Lee. U.A. Fanthorpe makes

good use of everyday language in her poem with phrases like 'that lot' and 'a laugh a minute'. Also in this poem it is clear to see that it is a poem about a child with the use of children's food like Coke and Kit-Kat. It uses quotes from the exam paper that the boy has done to show that he thought of Mr Lee's poetry in a different way to examiners. You can see that narrator has a certain amount of empathy with the poet Mr Lee by the lines 'I didn't think you'd want your book read that way'. This backs up the idea of the narrator seeing the enjoying properly as Mr Lee intended. ✓

Some good ideas and an attempt to engage with language and style.

15/25

Grade booster ····▷ move C to B

- More detailed references to the text needed.
- Ideas need developing in more detail.
- Technical accuracy needs attention.

GRADE A ANSWER

Sandra

Although Hugo Williams and U.A. Fanthorpe both present experiences of school life in their poems 'Leaving School' and 'Dear Mr Lee', the poems are quite different in tone.

Good focus on tone with some aptly supported analysis.

In 'Leaving School', a poem which depicts a child's experience of boarding school, the tone is quite sad. One of the ways the poet achieves this is through the images that he presents. ✓ For example, the boy appears to have been forced prematurely into the role of an adult as he 'set out into the world' at only eight years old. This suggestion is further enhanced when we read of his attire – 'a grey flannel suit' – thus projecting a somewhat uncomfortable, and inappropriate, image of the boy as a 'little man' ✓

Sensitive points with good textual support.

A degree of sadness is created as the boy is disillusioned – the 'new-found' independence which he 'thought would be fun' proved not to be so. The rest of the poem describes the restrictions – 'I could only read certain things', and isolation – 'I was miles away with my suitcase' that the child felt being away from home at boarding school. His suit, then, succeeds in reasserting this idea of 'restriction'. ✓

Perceptive points well put.

The 'alien' environment that the child finds himself in is one where he is punished and shamed for apparently trivial misdemeanours, 'Every day my name was read out because I had forgotten to hang something up'. ✓ Indeed, the alienation he feels is demonstrated by his forgetfulness; the apparent unfamiliarity of his surroundings causing him to express 'I was so far away from home I used to forget things.'

Some very thorough and detailed reading here.

Williams also succeeds in expressing a sense of the boy's fear by incorporating threatening, foreboding images in his poem. For example, he is told to think of the timetable as a game of 'Battleships', thus creating a sense of war. ✓ In addition, we are told that the headmaster's wife came round for 'inspection' – a word associated with the military – again reasserting the idea of war and, consequently, we are forced to see the boy's school environment in terms of a 'battlefield'. ✓

Begins to contrast with Fanthorpe's poem. Good contrast of tone, again well-supported.

In contrast, the tone in U.A. Fanthorpe's 'Dear Mr Lee' is quite comical. We are presented with a humorous attempt by a child to write to the author of his favourite book 'Cider With Rosie' by Laurie Lee. One of the ways Fanthorpe creates this humour is through the child's asides: '(Mr. Smart says it's rude to call you Laurie...)' ✓ and 'as for Shakespeare (we're doing him too)'. Fanthorpe's use of language also creates a comical effect. For example, the use of clichés – the child describes the works of Ted Hughes and Philip Larkin as not being 'a laugh a minute'. ✓

Continues to make detailed and perceptive points.

Fanthorpe also creates humour in adopting a childlike style in which to write the poem. For example, although a letter, the style of the poem does not conform to the formal structure expected within letter writing. ✓ Rather, the poem is written in a conversational style with elements of speech being in evidence. For instance, the 'letter' is started more than once, the poem is constructed of long sentences of weak grammatical structure and there is use of specific references and colloquial vocabulary: 'Ted Hughes and Philip Larkin and that lot.' In addition to creating humour, the chosen style is appropriate bearing in mind the narrator is a child. ✓

Although humorous, the poem 'Dear Mr Lee', like 'Leaving School', has a serious element to it. The underlying suggestion is that the book, which the child has apparently enjoyed and appreciated as a work of fiction, somehow loses its 'value' when the child is forced to view it from the different angles suggested by Mr Smart: 'social welfare in the rural community' and 'the seasons as perceived by an adolescent' ✓ – The teacher's name, Mr Smart, appearing somewhat ironic when taking this view – irony being another way in which Fanthorpe creates humour.

The poem appears to suggest that it is this work of fiction, rather than Mr Smart, which has enthused and inspired the child to read and learn further: 'I've got the next one out of the Public Library about Spain, and I asked Mum about learning to play the fiddle.' Fanthorpe appears to question the way that works of literature are approached and the effectiveness of teaching methods used in school. ✓ The constraints and ineffectiveness of the school environment in actually teaching children is also a suggestion in Hugo Williams's poem. The very title 'Leaving School' intimates that the boy has left the learning environment of 'home' to one where he 'said "I don't know" then...started saying nothing.' ✓

We can see, therefore, that, although both poems present experiences which cause us to question the effectiveness of 'school' as a learning environment, the manner in which these ideas are expressed differ in the two. Hugo Williams presents this idea somewhat more overtly in the distressing poem 'Leaving School', however Fanthorpe's comical approach in 'Dear Mr Lee' is also seriously thought provoking. ✓

22/25

Good point here.

Some explanation of this would be useful.

Not entirely clear.

Good point.

Overall some excellent points here with good textual support.

Writing on literary texts

Grade booster ···> move A to A*
The concluding points concerning the poem's purpose could be developed a little more clearly.

79

1 Read the poems 'Blackberrying' by Sylvia Plath and 'Blackberry-Picking' by Seamus Heaney. Compare and contrast the ways in which the two poets present the experience of blackberry picking and reveal their own thoughts and feelings.

In your answer you should consider closely the poets' use of language. ㉕

Blackberrying

Nobody in the lane, and nothing, nothing but blackberries,
Blackberries on either side, though on the right mainly,
A blackberry alley, going down in hooks, and a sea
Somewhere at the end of it, heaving. Blackberries
Big as the ball of my thumb, and dumb as eyes
Ebon in the hedges, fat
With blue-red juices. These they squander on my fingers.
I had not asked for such a blood sisterhood; they must love me.
They accommodate themselves to my milkbottle, flattening their sides.

Overhead go the choughs in black, cacophonous flocks –
Bits of burnt paper wheeling in a blown sky.
Theirs is the only voice, protesting, protesting.
I do not think the sea will appear at all.
The high, green meadows are glowing, as if lit from within.
I come to one bush of berries so ripe it is a bush of flies,
Hanging their bluegreen bellies and their wing panes in a Chinese screen.
The honey-feast of the berries has stunned them; they believe in heaven.
One more hook and the berries and bushes end.

The only thing to come now is the sea.
From between two hills a sudden wind funnels at me,
Slapping its phantom laundry in my face.
These hills are too green and sweet to have tasted salt.
I follow the sheep path between them. A lost hook brings me
To the hills' northern face, and the face is orange rock
That looks out on nothing, nothing but a great space
Of white and pewter lights, and a din like silversmiths
Beating and beating at an intractable metal.

Sylvia Plath

Blackberry-Picking
For Philip Hobsbaum

Late August, given heavy rain and sun
For a full week, the blackberries would ripen.
At first, just one, a glossy purple clot
Among others, red, green, hard as a knot.
You ate that first one and its flesh was sweet
Like thickened wine: summer's blood was in it
Leaving stains upon the tongue and lust for
Picking. Then red ones inked up and that hunger
Sent us out with milk-cans, pea-tins, jam-pots
Where briars scratched and wet grass bleached our boots.
Round hayfields, cornfields and potato-drills
We trekked and picked until the cans were full,
Until the tinkling bottom had been covered
With green ones, and on top big dark blobs burned
Like a plate of eye. Our hands were peppered
With thorn pricks, our palms sticky as Bluebeard's.

We hoarded the flesh berries in the byre.
But when the bath was filled we found a fur,
A rat-grey fungus, glutting on our cache.
The juice was stinking too. Once off the bush
The fruit fermented, the sweet flesh would turn sour.
I always felt like crying. It wasn't fair
That all the lovely canfuls smelt of rot.
Each year I hoped they'd keep, knew they would not.

Seamus Heaney

---

2 Read the poems 'Sonnet' by John Clare and 'Inversnaid' by Gerard Manley Hopkins. Compare the ways in which the two poets use language to present images of nature.

Sonnet

I love to see the summer beaming forth
And white wool sack clouds sailing to the north
I love to see the wild flowers come again
And Mare blobs stain with gold the meadow drain
And water lilies whiten on the floods
Where reed clumps rustle like a wind shook wood
Where from her hiding place the Moor Hen pushes
And seeks her flag nest floating in bull rushes
I like the willow leaning half way o'er
The clear deep lake to stand upon its shore
I love the hay grass when the flower head swings
To summer winds and insects' happy wings
That sport about the meadow the bright day
And see bright beetles in the clear lake play

John Clare (1841)

Inversnaid

This darksome burn, horseback brown,
His rollrock highroad roaring down,
In coop and in comb the fleece of his foam
Flutes and low to the lake falls home.

A windpuff-bonnet of fawn-froth
Turns and twindles over the broth
Of a pool so pitchblack, fell-frowning,
It rounds and rounds Despair to drowning.

Degged with dew, dappled with dew
Are the groins of the braes that the brook treads through,
Wiry heathpacks, flitches of fern,
And the beadbonny ash that sits over the burn.

What would the world be, once bereft
Of wet and of wildness? Let them be left,
O let them be left, wildness and wet;
Long live the weeds and the wilderness yet.

Gerard Manley Hopkins (1881)

---

3 Read 'Mirror' by Sylvia Plath and 'My Grandmother' by Elizabeth Jennings. Compare what the poets have to say about the ageing process and examine the ways in which they use language to achieve their effects.

Mirror

I am silver and exact. I have no preconceptions.
Whatever I see I swallow immediately
Just as it is, unmisted by love or dislike.
I am not cruel, only truthful –
The eye of a little god, four-cornered.
Most of the time I meditate on the opposite wall.
It is pink, with speckles. I have looked at it so long
I think it is part of my heart. But it flickers.
Faces and darkness separate us over and over.

Now I am a lake. A woman bends over me,
Searching my reaches for what she really is.
Then she turns to those liars, the candles or the moon.
I see her back, and reflect it faithfully.
She rewards me with tears and an agitation of hands.
I am important to her. She comes and goes.
Each morning it is her face that replaces the darkness.
In me she has drowned a young girl, and in me an old woman
Rises towards her day after day, like a terrible fish.

Sylvia Plath

My Grandmother

She kept an antique shop – or it kept her.
Among Apostle spoons and Bristol glass,
The faded silks, the heavy furniture,
She watched her own reflection in the brass
Salvers and silver bowls, as if to prove
Polish was all, there was no need of love.

And I remember how I once refused
To go out with her, since I was afraid.
It was perhaps a wish not to be used
Like antique objects. Though she never said
That she was hurt, I still could feel the guilt
Of that refusal, guessing how she felt.

Later, too frail to keep a shop, she put
All her best things in one long, narrow room.
The place smelt old, of things too long kept shut,
The smell of absences where shadows come
That can't be polished. There was nothing then
To give her own reflection back again.

And when she died I felt no grief at all,
Only the guilt of what I once refused.
I walked into her room among the tall
Sideboards and cupboards – things she never used
But needed: and no finger-marks were there,
Only the new dust falling through the air.

Elizabeth Jennings

Writing on literary texts

EXAMINER'S TIP

Poems can be open to many interpretations and so these kinds of questions do not have 'right' or 'wrong' answers but they do want you to explore your own ideas on the poems.

- *Read the poems through very carefully several times and try to form some ideas on them.*
- *Write in well-structured sentences, spelling and punctuation must be accurate.*
- *Focus on specific details of the ways in which the poets use language.*
- *Comment on the effectiveness of devices that might be used, such as metaphors, similes, alliteration, etc. Don't just identify them but explain the effects they create within the poem.*
- *Present your work well.*

① Here are some points you might have explored.
'Blackberrying'
- The repetition of blackberry/blackberries in the first stanza and the effect this creates.
- The imagery Plath uses to give an impression of the ripeness of the blackberries, for example the simile 'Big as the ball of my thumb' and the use of personification.
- The imagery used to describe the choughs (a bird that inhabits sea-cliffs, very like a crow but with a long, curved orange beak) – note the use of onomatopoeia and metaphors here.
- Plath uses colour in her poem to create different impressions – 'green', 'black', 'bluegreen', 'orange', 'white', 'pewter'. Comment on the effects created by these.
- You should also comment on the mood/atmosphere created.
'Blackberry Picking'
- Note the combination of rain/sun to help the blackberries ripen.
- The imagery used (both metaphors and similes) to give the impression of ripeness e.g. 'purple clot', 'hard as a knot', 'thickened wine', 'summer's blood', etc.
- The various items used to collect the blackberries.
- The description of the countryside – 'the briars', 'wet grass', 'potato-drills', etc.
- The juxtaposition of the wholesome fruitfulness of the berries and the fungus that grew on them when picked and stored that ends the poem.
- The significance of the last line.
Areas for comparison/contrast
- The poets' use of imagery
- The descriptions of the natural settings
- The mood/atmosphere created
- The structure of the poems

- The poets' attitude to the topic

EXAMINER'S TIP

Make sure that you support the points you make through clear, appropriate details from the poems and focus closely on the ways in which the poets use language to create their effects.

② **'Sonnet'**
- The poem is written in the first person and this gives a sense that the poet is addressing the reader directly.
- Look at the use of metaphor – e.g. 'white wool sack clouds', 'Mare blobs stain with gold'.
- The use of similes – 'reed clumps rustle like a wind shook wood'.
- The personification of nature – 'summer beaming forth'.
- The use of adjectives to intensify the effect of the description.
- The rhythm pattern of the poem.
- The effect of the rhyming couplets.
'Inversnaid'
- The use of alliteration, e.g. 'foam-froth', 'dappled with dew', etc.
- The use of vivid adjectives, e.g. 'darksome burn', 'horseback brown'.
- New words created by putting words together – e.g. 'rollrock', 'windpuff'.
- Coining of new words – e.g. 'degged', 'heath packs', 'twindles'.
- The atmosphere of wildness and darkness created.
- The structure of the poem in stanzas.
- The use of rhyming couplets.

③ **'Mirror'**
- It is important to recognise the use the poet makes of the metaphors of the mirror and the lake – both of which show reflections.
- The poem has a 'riddle-like' quality about it.
- The passing of time and ageing are important in the poem.
- The use of contrasts is important in creating effects.
- Metaphors and images are used.
- The final two lines carry the key message of the poem.
'My Grandmother'
- The poem reveals the granddaughter's feelings about her grandmother.
- The structure of the poem into four stanzas is important.
- The vocabulary is simple and straightforward.
- The poem presents a view of growing old.
- The rhyme scheme contributes to the overall effect.

CHAPTER 8

Writing on poems from different cultures

To revise this topic more thoroughly, see Chapter 11 in Letts *Revise GCSE English Guide.*

 Try this sample GCSE question and then compare your answer with the Grade C and Grade A model answers pages 88–90.

Read 'Presents from my Aunts in Pakistan' by Moniza Alvi and 'Hurricane Hits England' by Grace Nichols. Compare and contrast the ways in which the poets use language in these two poems to create a sense of their own confused identities and experiences.

Spend about 45 minutes on this.

Write about 300–400 words.

Leave enough time to read through and correct what you have written.

(25 marks)

Presents from my Aunts in Pakistan

They sent me a salwar kameez
   peacock-blue.
     and another
  glistening like an orange split open,
embossed slippers, gold and black
    points curling.
  Candy-striped glass bangles
    snapped, drew blood.
  Like at school, fashions changed
    in Pakistan –
the salwar bottoms were broad and stiff,
    then narrow.
My aunts chose an apple-green sari.
  silver-bordered
    for my teens.

I tried each satin-silken top –
   was alien in the sitting-room.
I could never be as lovely
     as those clothes –
   I longed
for denim and corduroy.

My costume clung to me
            and I was aflame,
I couldn't rise up out of its fire,
            half-English,
                        unlike Aunt Jamila.

I wanted my parents' camel-skin lamp –
            switching it on in my bedroom,
to consider the cruelty
                        and the transformation
from camel to shade,
            marvel at the colours
                        like stained glass.

My mother cherished her jewellery –
            Indian gold, dangling, filigree,
                        But it was stolen from our car.
The presents were radiant in my wardrobe.
            My aunts requested cardigans
                        from Marks and Spencers.
My salwar kameez
            didn't impress the schoolfriend
who sat on my bed, asked to see
            my weekend clothes.
But often I admired the mirror-work,
            tried to glimpse myself
                        in the miniature
glass circles, recall the story
            how the three of us
                        sailed to England.
Prickly heat had me screaming on the way.
            I ended up in a cot
in my English grandmother's dining-room,
            found myself alone,
                        playing with a tin boat.

I pictured my birthplace
            from fifties' photographs.
                        When I was older
there was conflict, a fractured land
            throbbing through newsprint.
Sometimes I saw Lahore –
                        my aunts in shaded rooms,
screened from male visitors,
            sorting presents,
                        wrapping them in tissue.

Or there were beggars, sweeper-girls
            and I was there –
                        of no fixed nationality,
staring through fretwork
            at the Shalimar Gardens.

Moniza Alvi

Hurricane Hits England

It took a hurricane, to bring her closer
To the landscape.
Half the night she lay awake,
The howling ship of the wind,
Its gathering rage,
Like some dark ancestral spectre.

Talk to me Huracan
Talk to me Oya
Talk to me Shango
And Hattie,
My sweeping, back-home cousin.

Tell me why you visit
An English coast?
What is the meaning
Of old tongues
Reaping havoc
In new places?

The blinding illumination,
Even as you short-
Circuit us
Into further darkness?

What is the meaning of trees
Falling heavy as whales
Their crusted roots
Their cratered graves?

O why is my heart unchained?

Tropical Oya of the Weather,
I am aligning myself to you,
I am following the movement of your winds,
I am riding the mystery of your storm.

Ah, sweet mystery,
Come to break the frozen lake in me,
Shaking the foundations of the very trees within me,
Come to let me know
That the earth is the earth is the earth.

Grace Nichols

These two answers are at grades C and A. Compare which one your answer is closest to and think how you could have improved it.

GRADE C ANSWER

SPELLCHECK!

receiving
family
as if
apostrophe
has followed

Brief introduction sets the poem in context.

Close reading of poem with supporting examples.

A good point – shows perception here.

Can see the idea but not well put.

Again not very clearly put.

An interesting comment.

Brings in an element of comparison.

There are some good ideas here but they remain undeveloped.

Gemma

When receving presents from my Aunts in Pakistan I can see that the poem is relating to a girl that has moved from Pakistan to England. Her Aunts still live in Pakistan and visit every so often.

When they visit they bring presents for her and her family. ✓

They bought the girl a salwar kameez, gold slippers and bangles the salwar kameez was peacock blue and another 'glistening like an orange split ✓ open.' Which are very alien to her as all in her wardrobe were a lot of denim and all colour but that is what she wanted.

It also says that when her Aunts visit they request cardigans from Marks and Spencers which is a comparison as her Aunts are making her into an Indian girl but her Aunts want to wear English ✓ clothes. It is has if the girl has been torn in half between her two cultures as she is not part of one culture and she is not part of another.

The other poem I looked at was Hurricane Hits England. In this poem I can see that she has moved from one place to another England in this case and it is as if the hurricane has followed her. The poem has a bit of a ghostly form inside it 'like some dark ancestral spectre'. There is also aprostify as she is talking to the hurricanes. It is has if the hurricane as followed her to England. 'The blinding illumination' like the truth is blinding and how it is shocking. Right at the very end of the poem the hurricane has come to let her know ✓ that she is still part of the Earth she came from.

The comparisons in these two poems are that both main people in the story have moved from one place to another. I think that the girl in Presents from my Aunts in Pakistan is not as cut up about moving from her old house as the other girl is in Hurricane Hits England.

13/25

Grade booster ···⟩ move C to B
- Greater development of ideas and more specific examples from the poems to support them.
- More comment on the ways in which the language works in the poems.
- Attention to technical accuracy.

Writing on poems from different cultures

Doesn't comment on effects.

Begins a close reading and makes some perceptive comments here.

Good point.

Sees the link between the two poems and makes a valid comparison.

Uses example from the poem and some comment on its effect.

similes
alliteration
decisions
philosophical
where
demons
Whereas
commenting
things
the poets

Interesting and perceptive point.

Some valid contrast/comparison points here.

Andy

Presents From my Aunts in Pakistan.
In this poem the poet Moniza Alvi uses simlies
metaphor allteration and assonance. Moniza talks
about fitting in with our English society and how
different it is from her own culture back in
Pakistan. Line 7 of the poem she talks about
the 'candy striped glass bangles snapped, drew
blood'. This would insinuate something so beautiful
like candy has hurt her, drawn blood. This would
also say to me that they did not fit and that
is why they broke. ✓ Like again stating it does
not fit and neither does this new culture ✓ or
way of living. Line 13 she says that her aunts
still have a big hold over her and the disicitions
that she makes. The clothes that are fashionable
in Pakistan are not fashionable in England but
she will still defend the right to wear them. ✓

The Hurricane Hits England is also about the
poet's confused identity. Grace Nichols talks
about the journey to England being a rougher
ride. I think that she feels a lot stronger about
leaving her home land to come to England than
Moniza Alvi does. Moniza's main focus is about
her clothes, fashion and just trying to fit in.
Grace Nichols is a lot more philosopical in her
expressions. Take line 4 of the poem were she
uses the phrase howling ship. This is a metaphor
because it is very rare that you would ever hear
a ship howl. Hurricane Hits England seems to me
to be a lot more of a sombre poem than Moniza.
Line 6 of Grace's poem she writes 'like some
dark ancestral spectre' this would tell me that
something very bad is on its way if not it has
already arrived. Grace's poem is more about
wrestling the demon's inside. ✓ Where as Moniza's
poem is somenting on the thing's that are
happening around her.

Both of the poems have a different pace to
them and a different outcome even though they
poet's are talking about the same subject. Grace
Nichols is very aware of the old customs and
rules of her former country, ✓ and saying on the

Good – relevant and focused comment.

Sums up ideas to conclude. Lots of personal engagement here – close reading and good use of text.

last paragraph that they are still very much part of who she really is. Grace Nichols is questioning her move to England in an inner spiritual sort of sense. ✓ Grace Nichols has moved away from her home land but is still aware of who she is and where she has come from. Moniza is bewildered with her two cultures. ✓ The culture of her aunts from Pakistan and the culture of her friends from school. Moniza is torn like the old expression 'Caught between a rock and a hard place' where as Grace Nichols just feels sad for what she has left behind.

In conclusion to both of the poems I have read. I would say both of the authors are talking about their confused identities. Grace Nichols makes alot more references to her inner self and in a way, what her soul is feeling where as Moniza Alvi uses more comparisons to objects and items of clothing.

21/25

Grade booster ⋯⋟ move A to A*
- Some of the ideas could be developed in greater depth and the comments focus on the **effects** of the language features identified as well as describing them.
- Attention should be paid to technical accuracy.

Spend about 45 minutes on each of the questions in this section.

1 Read 'Fantasy of an African Boy' by James Berry and 'Blessing' by Imtiaz Dharker. Compare and contrast the ways in which each poet uses language to convey a sense of the needs and lives of the peoples they describe. ㉕

Fantasy of an African Boy

Such a peculiar lot
we are, we people
without money, in daylong
yearlong sunlight, knowing
money is somewhere, somewhere.

Everybody says it's a big
bigger brain bother now,
money. Such millions and millions
of us don't manage at all
without it our heads alone
stay big, as lots and lots do,
coming from nowhere joyful,
going nowhere happy.

We can't drink it up. Yet
Without it we shrivel when small
And stop forever
Where we stopped,
As lots and lots do.

We can't read money for books.
Yet without it we don't
read, don't write numbers,
don't open gates in other countries,
as lots and lots never do.

We can't use money to bandage
Sores, can't pound it
to powder for sick eyes
and sick bellies. Yet without
it, flesh melts from our bones.

Such walled-round gentlemen
overseas minding money! Such
bigtime gentlemen, body guarded
because of too much respect
and too many wishes on them:

too many wishes, everywhere,
wanting them to let go
magic of money, and let it fly
away, everywhere, day and night,
just like dropped leaves in the wind!

James Berry

Blessing

The skin cracks like a pod.
There never is enough water.

Imagine the drip of it,
the small splash, echo
in a tin mug,
the voice of a kindly God.

Sometimes, the sudden rush
of fortune. The municipal pipe bursts,
silver crashes to the ground
and the flow has found
a roar of tongues. From the huts,
a congregation: every man woman
child for streets around
butts in, with pots,
brass, copper, aluminium,
plastic buckets,
frantic hands,

and naked children
screaming in the liquid sun,
their highlights polished to perfection,
flashing light,
as the blessing sings
over their small bones.

Imtiaz Dharker

---

2 Read 'Sugar Cane' by Grace Nichols and 'French Colonial' by Margaret Atwood. Compare and contrast the ways in which the poets explore their ideas and use language to achieve their effects.

㉕

Sugar Cane

1

There is something
about sugar cane

he isn't what
he seem –

indifferent hard
and sheathed in blades

his waving arms
is a sign for help

his skin thick
only to protect
the juice inside
himself

2

His colour
is the aura
of jaundice
when he ripe

he shiver
like the ague
when it rain

he suffer
from bellywork
burning fever
and delirium

just before
the hurricane
strike
smashing him to pieces

3

Growing up
is an art

he don't have
any control of

it is us
who groom and
weed him

who stick him
in the earth
in the first place

and when he
growing tall

with the help
of the sun
and rain

we feel the
need to strangle
the life

out of him

But either way he
  can't survive

4

Slowly
pain –
fully
sugar
cane
pushes
his
knotted
joints
upwards
from
the

earth
slowly
pain –
fully
he
comes
to learn
the
truth
about
himself
the
crimes
committed
in
his
name

5

He cast his shadow
to the earth

the wind is
his only mistress

I hear them
moving
in rustling tones

she shakes
his hard reserve

smoothing
stroking
caressing
all his length
shamelessly

I crouch
below them
quietly
           Grace Nichols

French Colonial

This was a plantation once,
owned by a Frenchman. The well survives,
filled now with algae, heartcoloured
dragonflies, thin simmer of mosquitoes.

Here is an archway, grown over
with the gross roots of trees,
here's a barred window,
a barn or prison.
Fungus blackens the wall
as if they're burned, but no need:
thickening vines lick over
and through them, a slow
green fire. Sugar,
it was then. Now there are rows
of yellowing limes, the burrows
of night crabs. Five hundred yards
away, seared women in flowered dresses
heap plates at the buffet.
We'll soon join them.
The names of the bays:
Hope, Friendship and Industry.

The well is a stone hole
opening out of the darkness,
drowned history. Who knows
what's down there? How many
spent lives, killed muscles.
It's the threshold of an unbuilt
house. We sit on the rim
in the sun, talking
of politics. You could still
drink the water.

Margaret Atwood

---

3 Compare the ways in which the poets present their ideas in 'Vultures' by Chinua Achebe and 'Not My Business' by Niyi Osundare.

Vultures

In the greyness
and drizzle of one despondent
dawn unstirred by harbingers
of sunbreak a vulture
perching high on broken
bone of a dead tree
nestled close to his
mate his smooth
bashed-in head, a pebble
on a stem rooted in
a dump of gross
feathers, inclined affectionately

to hers. Yesterday they picked
the eyes of a swollen
corpse in a water-logged
trench and ate the
things in its bowel. Full
gorged they chose their roost
keeping the hollowed remnant
in easy range of cold
telescopic eyes...
Strange
indeed how love in other
ways so particular
will pick a corner
in that charnel-house
tidy it and coil up there, perhaps
even fall asleep – her face
turned to the wall!
...Thus the Commandant at Belsen
Camp going home for
the day with fumes of
human roast clinging
rebelliously to his hairy
nostrils will stop
at the wayside sweet-shop
and pick up a chocolate
for his tender offspring
waiting at home for Daddy's
return...
Praise bounteous
providence if you will
that grants even an ogre
a tiny glow-worm
tenderness encapsulated
in icy caverns of a cruel
heart or else despair
for in the very germ
of that kindred love is
lodged the perpetuity
of evil.

Chinua Achebe

Not my Business

They picked Akanni up one morning
Beat him soft like clay
And stuffed him down the belly
Of a waiting jeep.
    What business of mine is it
    So long they don't take the yam
    From my savouring mouth?

They came one night
Booted the whole house awake
And dragged Danladi out,
Then off to a lengthy absence.
    What business of mine is it
    So long they don't take the yam
    From my savouring mouth?

Chinwe went to work one day
Only to find her job was gone:
No query, no warning, no probe –
Just one neat sack for a stainless record.
    What business of mine is it
    So long they don't take the yam
    From my savouring mouth?

And then one evening
As I sat down to eat my yam
A knock on the door froze my hungry hand.
The jeep was waiting on my bewildered lawn
Waiting, waiting in its usual silence.

Niyi Osundare

ANSWERS ON PAGE 97 ANSWERS ON PAGE 97 ANSWERS ON PAGE 97 ANSWERS ON PAGE 97

QUESTION BANK ANSWERS

① **'Fantasy of an African Boy'**
- Note the use of 'we' – the poet is including himself as one of the people he is describing.
- The sense of the hot climate stressed by 'daylong/yearlong' sunlight.
- Repetition of 'money' stressing that, although intrinsically it is of no value (e.g. 'We can't drink it up', 'we can't read money for books' etc.) but it buys what is essential for survival.
- A sense of deprivation is emphasised through phrases like 'coming from nowhere joyful/going to nowhere happy', 'we shrivel when small', 'sick eyes', 'sick bellies', 'flesh melts from our bones', etc.
- Contrast created through the description of the deprivation lack of money causes and the wealth that some people possess (e.g. 'walled-round gentlemen/overseas minding money!').

'Blessing'
- The opening simile creates a sense of the dry and parched – 'The skin cracks like a pod'.
- The poem is written in the third person.
- Images stress the precious nature of water ('Imagine the drip of it…the voice of a kindly God.')
- The description of the people rushing for water when a pipe bursts again stresses the scarcity and precious nature of water.

- Images such as 'the liquid sun', 'flashing light' creates a sense of the life-giving qualities of water.
- 'Naked children', 'their small bones' create a sense of innocence and vulnerability of the children who play in the flowing water.

② **'Sugar Cane'**
- the personification of the sugar cane, e.g. 'his waving arms', 'he shivers', etc. creates a sense of the sugar cane as a living, feeling being.
- The ambiguity of the sugar cane is stressed, 'he isn't what/he seem'.
- The language gives a sense of a dialect form but without dominating the poem – e.g. 'he seem', 'when he ripe', 'he suffer', 'he don't have', etc. which gives a sense of the poetic voice behind the poem.
- The structure of the poem with very short lines, particularly in stanza 4, gives a physical impression of the tall, slender sugar cane pushing up through the earth.

'French Colonial'
- The poem reflects on the past, 'This was a plantation once'.
- A sense of heat is created through 'this simmer of mosquitoes'.
- There is a sense of decay and things being overgrown suggested by words such as 'grown over', 'fungus blackens the walls', 'thickening vines', etc.
- The past history of the sugar cane plantation and the suffering of the slaves who worked it under their colonial masters is suggested through 'damned history', 'spent lives', 'killed muscles'.
- The irony of the names of the bays, 'Hope', 'Friendship', 'Industry'.

❸ **'Vultures'**

- The atmosphere created by the negative language, e.g. 'greyness', 'drizzle', 'broken bone', 'dead tree', etc.
- The graphic, uncompromising images created by powerful language, e.g. 'picked the eyes of a swollen / corpse'.
- The use of enjambment to build one image upon another.
- The structure of the poem – the relationship between the first part of the poem and the second part which begins 'Thus the Commandant...'
- The message of the poem encapsulated in the closing lines 'In the very germ / of that kindred love is / lodged the perpetuity / of evil'.

'Not My Business'

- The use of imagery, e.g. 'beat him soft like clay'.
- The use of the refrain – 'What business of mine is it / So long they don't take the yam / From my savouring mouth?' sets up the message of the poem.
- The link between this refrain and the final stanza makes the poet's message clear.
- The poem is structured in stanzas each of which contains a 'story' in its own right but which link together.
- The poet uses the first person and so is involved and eventually a victim of the situation described.

Centre number	
Candidate number	
Surname and initials	

Examining Group

General Certificate of Secondary Education

English
Paper 1

For Examiner's use only	
1	
2	
3	
4	
5	
6	
7	
Total	

Time: one and a half hours

Instructions to candidates

- Answer **two** questions. Answer **one** question from Section A (Non-fiction/media texts) and **one** question from Section B (Writing to argue/persuade/advise).
- Spend about **45 minutes** on Section A and about **45 minutes** on Section B.
- You must **not** use a dictionary in this examination.

Information for candidates

- The number of marks is given in brackets at the end of each question.

EDUCATIONAL

SECTION A

Leave blank

- Answer **one** question from this section (Non fiction/media texts). Answer **both** parts (**a** and **b**) of the question you choose.
- Spend about 45 minutes on this section.

EITHER

Question 1

The following extract is from *A Walk in the Woods* by Bill Bryson. This book gives an account of his journey with his friend, Katz, along the Appalachian Trail in the United States, the longest continuous footpath in the world. Read it through carefully and then answer the questions that follow it.

(a) Summarise what you learn about Bryson's feelings about woods from this extract. You should write approximately 150–200 words. **[10]**

(b) Examine the ways in which Bryson uses language to achieve his effects here.
[15]
(Total 25 marks)

100

A Walk in the Woods

Woods are not like other spaces. To begin with they are cubic. Their trees surround you, loom over you, press in from all sides. Woods choke off views, and leave you muddled and without bearings. They make you feel small and confused and vulnerable, like a small child lost in a crowd of strange legs. Stand in a desert or prairie and you know you are in a big space. Stand in a wood and you only sense it. They are a vast, featureless nowhere. And they are alive.

So woods are spooky. Quite apart from the thought that they may harbour wild beasts and armed, genetically challenged fellows named Zeke and Festus, there is something innately sinister about them – some ineffable thing that makes you sense an atmosphere of pregnant doom with every step and leaves you profoundly aware that you are out of your element and ought to keep your ears pricked. Though you tell yourself it's preposterous, you can't quite shake the feeling that you are being watched. You order yourself to be serene – it's just a wood for goodness' sake – but really you are jumpier than Don Knotts with pistol drawn. Every sudden noise – the crack of a falling limb, the crash of a bolting deer – makes you spin in alarm and stifle a plea for mercy. Whatever mechanism within you is responsible for adrenaline, it has never been sleek and polished – so keenly poised to pump out a warming squirt of adrenal fluid. Even asleep you are a coiled spring.

The American woods have been unnerving people for 300 years. The inestimably priggish and tiresome Henry David Thoreau thought nature was splendid, splendid indeed, so long as he could stroll to town for cakes and barley wine, but when he experienced real wilderness, on a visit to Katahdin in 1846, he was unnerved to the core. This wasn't the tame world of overgrown orchards and sun-dappled paths that passed for wilderness in suburban Concord, Massachusetts, but a forbidding, oppressive, primeval country that was 'grim and wild…savage and dreary', fit only for 'men nearer of kin to the rocks and wild animals than we'. The experience left him in the words of one biographer, 'near hysterical'.

But even men far tougher and more attuned to the wilderness than Thoreau were sobered by its strange and palpable menace. Daniel Boone, who not only wrestled bears but tried to date their sisters, described corners of the southern Appalachians as 'so wild and horrid that it is impossible to behold them without terror'. When Daniel Boone is uneasy, you know it is time to watch your step.

When the first Europeans arrived in the New World there were perhaps 950 million acres of woodland in what would become the lower forty-eight states. The Chattahoochee National Forest through which Katz and I now trudged was part of an immense unbroken canopy stretching from southern Alabama to Canada and beyond, and from the shores of the Atlantic to the distant grasslands of the Missouri River.

Most of that forest is now gone, but what survives is more impressive than you might expect. The Chattahoochee is part of four million acres – 6,000 square miles – of federally owned forest stretching up to the Great Smokey Mountains and beyond, and spreading sideways across four states. On a map of the United States it is an incidental smudge of green, but on foot the scale of it is colossal. It would be four days before Katz and I crossed a public highway, eight days till we came to a town.

And so we walked. We walked up mountains and through high, forgotten hollows, along lonesome ridges with long views of more ridges, over grassy balds and down rocky, twisting, jarring descents, and through mile after endless mile of dark, deep, silent woods, on a wandering trail eighteen inches wide and marked with rectangular white blazes (two inches wide, six long) slapped at intervals on the grey-barked trees. Walking is what we did.

[turn over

HOME HELP

If your child is the bully

• Make it clear that you love your child; it is the bullying behaviour you want changed

• Discuss with your child how they think they might change their behaviour and what help they might need to do so. If they are part of a group that is bullying they may be under pressure and worried that they will be bullied too

• Young children, especially, need to be told that hurting another child is not acceptable. Help them learn that using threats and force is not the way to get what they want. Older children need to be told that name calling, nasty teasing, spreading rumours about someone or ignoring someone all the time are all forms of bullying, as well as physical things like kicking or hitting or damaging possessions

• Help your child develop a feeling of what it might be like for others. Being sensitive to your child's needs will help learn about being sensitive to others

• Bullying is sometimes attention-seeking behaviour. Show your child approval just for being who they are, take an interest in them and show that you notice them when they are doing kind and positive things, not just when they are being 'naughty'

• Your child could be deeply frustrated with school work and taking their frustration out on others. They could be struggling with a condition such as dyslexia, for example, that has not been diagnosed. Help them get the help they need from the school

• Your child could be feeling very unhappy or insecure. Talk through any family problems that might be affecting them

• Children who bully are often suffering low self-esteem. Give your child love and reassurance rather than criticism, and do things that will help build self-esteem, such as making them feel special.

FURTHER HELP

Online and offline

Parentline Plus has a free helpline: 0808 800 2222 offering support for parents, or see their website: www.parentlineplus.org.uk

Don't Suffer in Silence is a leaflet full of advice for parents.
Call 0845 602 2260 for your copy or visit www.dontsufferinsilence.com
The BBC offers helpful advice at www.bbc.co.uk/education/archive/bully
Anti-Bullying Campaign – a parents' pack is available for £2.50 by sending an A4 SAE, two first class stamps and a cheque, or postal order made payable to Anti-Bullying Campaign to 185, Tower Bridge Road, London SE1 7UF Tel: 020 7378 1446

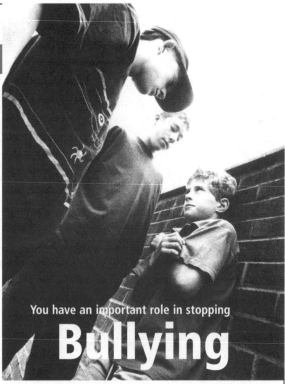

You have an important role in stopping
Bullying

No one likes a bully, and we've all heard stories of the long-lasting misery and harm it can cause. But what if the worst happens and you discover that it's your child who has been accused of bullying?

You have an important role in helping them stop this behaviour, and may find it useful to try out some of the following suggestions from parents' organisation Parentline Plus.

Obviously, you will want to tell your child that bullying is totally unacceptable behaviour and has to stop.

But if you tell your child off without listening to their side of the story, they are more likely to sulk, rebel or ignore you.

You may want to punish your child, but punishment is not usually enough to change behaviour.

However angry or upset you may feel, try to avoid losing your temper or being violent with your child – this could just make matters worse. If necessary, get support for yourself by talking to a friend or relative, or telephoning a helpline, such as the Parentline Plus free helpline on 0808 800 2222, before sitting down with your child to discuss what has happened.

You may think there is no problem – that it's just a 'bit of teasing' – or that it's natural for children to fight one another – not so. What may seem normal behaviour to you and your child could cause much distress to others.

And if it isn't dealt with quickly, it could lead to your child getting into trouble with the school and other authorities later on.

OR

Question 2

The article opposite is aimed at parents and deals with the issue of bullying. Read it carefully and then answer the following questions.

(a) Summarise the key points made in the article. You should write approximately 150–200 words. **[10]**

(b) Examine the ways in which ideas are conveyed in this article and comment on how effective you found it overall. **[15]**

(Total 25 marks)

In your answer you might comment on:

- the content of the article
- the use of headlines, sub-headings, pictures, etc.
- the layout and design
- the use of language
- any other features.

[turn over

SECTION B

- Answer **one** question from this section (Writing to argue/persuade/advise).
- Spend about 45 minutes on this section.

EITHER

Question 1

Write an article for a school or college magazine in which you argue that more facilities and equipment should be provided to ensure students receive the utmost from their studies.

You might consider some of the following:

- sports facilities
- computer-based facilities
- cafeteria/catering arrangements
- trips/travel opportunities
- other extra-curricular activities.

(25 marks)

OR

Question 2

Write an article for a village magazine in which you persuade the reader of the benefits of having a home computer. Your article should be aimed at an audience who are not very computer-literate.

(25 marks)

Letts Examining Group

General Certificate of Secondary Education

English
Paper 2

Time: one and a half hours

Instructions to candidates

- Answer **two** questions. Answer **one** question from Section A (Poems from different cultures) and **one** question from Section B (Writing to inform/explain/describe)
- Spend about **45 minutes** on Section A and about **45 minutes** on Section B.
- You must **not** use a dictionary in this examination.

Information for candidates

- The number of marks is given in brackets at the end of each question.

EDUCATIONAL

SECTION A

- There is **one** question in this section (Writing on poems from different cultures). Answer **both** parts of it.
- Spend about 45 minutes on this section.

Question 1

Read the following two poems which both describe storms. The first poem is by the American poet, Theodore Roethke, and the second one is by the Nigerian poet, Isaac I. Elimimian.

Compare and contrast the ways in which the poets create a sense of the storms and make them vivid for their readers.

You should refer to specific examples of the ways in which language is used to support your ideas.

(25 marks)

The Storm

Against the stone breakwater,
Only an ominous lapping,
While the wind whines overhead,
Coming down from the mountain,
Whistling between the arbours, the winding terraces;
A thin whine of wires, a rattling and flapping of leaves,
And the small streetlamp swinging and slamming against
   the lamp-pole.
Where have all the people gone?
There is one light on the mountain,
Along the sea-wall a steady sloshing of the swell,
The waves not yet high, but even,
Coming closer and closer upon each other;
A fine fume of rain driving in from the sea,
Riddling the sand, like a wide spray of buckshot,
The wind from the sea and the wind from the
   mountain contending,
Flicking the foam from the whitecaps straight upwards
   into the darkness.
A time to go home!
And a child's dirty shift billows upward out of an alley;
A cat runs from the wind as we do,
Between the whitening trees, up Santa Lucia,
Where the heavy door unlocks
And our breath comes more easy,
Then a crack of thunder, and the black rain runs
   over us, over
The flat-roofed houses, coming down in gusts, beating
The walls, the slatted windows, driving
The last watcher indoors, moving the cardplayers closer
To their cards, their Lachryma Christi.
We creep to our bed and its straw mattress.
We wait, we listen.
The storm lulls off, then redoubles,
Bending the trees halfway down to the ground,
Shaking loose the last wizened oranges in the orchard,
Flattening the limber carnations.
A spider eases himself down from a swaying light bulb,
Running over the coverlet, down under the iron bedstead.
The bulb goes on and off, weakly.
Water roars in the cistern.
We lie closer on the gritty pillow,
Breathing heavily, hoping –
For the great last leap of the wave over the breakwater,
The flat broom on the beach of the towering sea-swell,
The sudden shudder as the jutting sea-cliff collapses
And the hurricane drives the dead straw into the
   living pine-tree.

Theodore Roethke

[turn over

An African Downpour

One o'clock
Pom kpa kpa pom kpa kpa…
The rain fires its gun
Against enormous clouds of dust
And smoke
Flaming out the blast furnace
Intruding upon the smoky chimneys
Pacifying the chemical burnings
Warning the burnt out atmosphere.

Pom kpa kpa pom kpa kpa…
Rapping forward the debris
Heavily down the street highway
Rocking the baby in cradle bed
Scattering frustrated crowds at bus-stop
Setting drivers free from police traffic
Bringing hawking business down in one swoop
Dirt and grime taint red the walls

Pom kpa kpa pom kpa kpa
The flamboyant prostitute waits anxiously
Raising eyebrows for some brazen cab.

Two o'clock
Pom kpa kpa pom kpa kpa…
The wind and swish of lightning flash
Dismiss the blacksmith from the bellows
Killing the clank and thud of hammer
Sparks out the sleeping street lights
An old woman is struck dead

Pom kpa kpa pom kpa kpa…
The pools manager has not received the sporting record
The magistrate's car has no wiper
The rain blows the market stalls
The street ceremonies are dismissed
Beggars evacuate the open streets

Three o'clock
Pom kpa kpa pom kpa kpa…
The rain drones away
The odour of dank rotting refuse
The rancid black dregs down Musa street
The council scavengers are happy.

Pom kpa kpa pom kpa kpa
The mud-built walls give way
Lottery canvassers pack up
Vendors' magazines swim in muddy flood paddies
The cattle are grazing in the open fields

Four o'clock
The sky is bright and clear
Ditches roar with dynamic swift moves
Bootless father hugs Tom about the street
Couples are cowering indoors bobbing in love
School children push away sunken cars
Tomato seller cries out:
'Who will buy all these?'

Isaac I. Elimimian

SECTION B

- Answer **one** question from this section (Writing to inform/explain/describe).
- Spend about 45 minutes on this section.

EITHER

Question 1

You intend to start a new school club or society of your choice and have called an introductory meeting to explain your ideas. Write down what you would say at the meeting.

You might like to think about the following ideas:

- the kind of club/society you are starting
- the kinds of activities, etc. that will take place
- organisation issues
- membership arrangements
- any other ideas you think important.

(25 marks)

OR

Question 2

Write a description of a concert, play or sporting event that you have attended.

(25 marks)

[turn over

Answers to mock examination papers

Paper 1

Section A
Question 1

(a) Here are some key ideas you might have noted.

- Woods are different from other spaces because they make you feel small and vulnerable.
- They make you feel like a lost child.
- They are alive.
- They disorientate you so that you lose your bearings.
- They may contain wild animals and other dangers.
- They make you feel that you are being watched and make you feel on edge.
- Real wild woods are forbidding and unnerving places and every little noise can seem alarming.
- They are impressive.

(b)

- He creates a sense of the oppressive quality of woods through words and phrases such as 'surround you', 'loom over you', 'press in', 'choke', 'muddled', etc.
- He creates a sense of how they make you feel through words and phrases such as 'make you feel small', 'confused', 'vulnerable', 'like a small child'.
- He personifies the wood, making it seem like a living being – 'surround you', 'loom over you', 'pressing in on you', 'choking off views', etc.
- He uses historical references to illustrate the effect the wild woods can have on an individual.
- He uses humour through his reference to Daniel Boone to further illustrate the frightening nature of these places – e.g. 'when Daniel Boone is uneasy, you know it is time to watch your step.'
- He often uses short sentences that sum up key ideas, e.g. 'Woods are not like other spaces', 'So woods are spooky' or 'And they are alive'.

- He structures the writing so that he begins talking about the nature of woods and the effects they have on the mind, he goes on to illustrate this idea through historical references, gives background information on the Chattahoochee Forest he and Katz are walking through and ends with some specific details of the terrain they walked through.

Question 2
(a)

- The article focuses on the ways to help parents to discourage their children from bullying others.
- It is important how a parent tells a child that bullying is unacceptable and must stop.
- If it is handled wrongly the child may rebel and matters can be made worse.
- Punishment is not normally enough to change the behaviour of a child who has started bullying.
- Parents should avoid losing their temper or being violent with a child.
- It can help to get the support of a friend or relative.
- The issues need discussing with the child.
- If it isn't dealt with quickly it could lead to more problems later.

(b)

- The headline captures how parents usually react when they learn that their child is bullying.
- The sub-heading makes clear what the article aims to do.
- The language of the article is clear, straightforward and practical.
- A helpline telephone number is given.
- The bullet-points box gives a range of ideas about the issue, not only giving advice to parents but information on why a child might start to bully others.
- The Further Help box gives a range of information about where further help can be sought.

Section B
Question 1

- Your response should be in the form of an article.
- Your style and tone should be appropriate to a school or college magazine.
- The main point of your writing should be to provide arguments to justify the provision of more facilities and equipment.
- You should make specific points to support your ideas.
- You should structure your work effectively and present your ideas clearly.

Question 2

- Your response should be in the form of an article.
- Your style and tone should be appropriate for a village magazine.
- You should use your information persuasively to convince your readers of the value of a home computer.
- You should use specific examples and ideas of the uses to which home computers can be put, to make your piece more persuasive.
- Structure your work carefully and present your ideas clearly and accurately.

Paper 2

Section A
Question 1
'The Storm'

- 'Ominous' to describe the water lapping at the breakwater, signals the approaching storm and creates an atmosphere of expectation.
- The description of the wind helps to develop this atmosphere further – note the repetition of 'whine/whines'.
- The alliterative effect of 'wind whines', 'whistling…winding', 'whine of wires', 'small streetlamp swinging and slamming', 'steady sloshing of the swell', helps create a sense of the sound of wind and water.
- The descriptive detail of the sea state builds up the atmosphere – 'waves not yet high, but even / Coming closer and closer upon each other.'
- The use of metaphor and simile to increase the impact of the descriptive detail, e.g. 'Riddling the sand, like a wide spray of buckshot.'
- Note the close attention to small details such as the 'child's dirty shift', and the cat running from the wind.
- The detailed description of the storm as it breaks, with the focus on wind and rain.

- The contrast with people huddling in their beds again with a close attention to details such as the spider coming down from the swaying light bulb and running over the coverlet.

'An African Downpour'

- This poem contains a good deal of descriptive detail too.
- Note the use of metaphor, e.g. 'The rain fires its gun', 'Vendors' magazines swim in muddy flood paddies'.
- There is detailed description of the streets and the human life there, e.g. 'the baby in the cradle bed', 'The flamboyant prostitute'.
- The destructive power of the lightning is described, 'Killing the clank and thud of hammer', 'An old woman is struck dead'.
- Notice the emphasis on the dirt and grime of the town – 'Dirt and grime taint red walls', 'The odour of dank rotting refuse', etc.
- Note the description as the storm passes over.

Both poems

- Both poems describe storms but they take place in different countries and at different times of the day.
- Both poets make use of detailed description and close observation to bring their poems to life.
- The settings of the two poems are quite different.
- 'An African Downpour' also describes the scene after the storm has passed over.

Section B
Question 1

- You should be aware that you are going to be speaking to a group of people who might be interested in your club.
- You should cover the full range of information that you think people will want to know (use of the bullet point list should have helped here).
- You might organise your ideas under sub-headings to make the points more clearly.
- You should use an appropriate tone – remember that you are trying to get people interested and enthusiastic about your ideas.

Question 2

- Description based on personal experience can help to make your writing more vivid and convincing.
- Your work should focus on the vivid description of the experience.
- Small details can help to bring your writing to life and make it more 'real' to the reader.

111

Index

Acknowledgements: Brochure, by kind permission of The Welsh Highland Railway, Porthmadog; A Curlew in the Foreground © Philip Coxon, c/o David and Charles plc; The Migration, from My Family and Other Animals © Gerald Durrell c/o Curtis Brown Ltd; The complete beginners column, © Writing Magazine December 1995-January 1996; My best teacher – Errol Brown © John Guy, TES Friday 1/2/02; photo p39, © Barclay Graham/Corbis Sygma, Corbis Images; Illustration, Petrifying Truth, © Daniel Cookney, Text, Petrifying Truth, © David Windass, courtesy of Big Issue in the North; Penguins die in ice limbo © Jonathan Leake, Times Newspapers Limited; photo p.51,© RSPB; Dumfries and Galloway brochure, by kind permission of Richard Harris, DraftWorldwide; Brochure, © Friends of the Earth; Putting the Life Back, © Bird Magazine; photos pp.60, 61, © RSPB; An Evil Cradling by Brian Keenan, published by Hutchinson. Reprinted by permission of The Random House Group Ltd; All rights reserved; Vicious Circles, © Guy de la Bédoyere, Heritage Today, Dec 2001; Leaving School, © Hugo Williams; Dear Mr Lee, © U.A. Fanthorpe, A Watching Brief, 1987, Peterloo Poets; Blackberrying, © The Estate of Sylvia Plath, c/o Faber and Faber Ltd; Blackberry-Picking, © Seamus Heaney, c/o Faber and Faber Ltd; Sonnet, by John Clare, © Professor Robinson; Inversnaid, © Gerard Manley Hopkins; Mirror, © The Estate of Sylvia Plath, c/o Faber and Faber Ltd; My grandmother, © Elizabeth Jennings, c/o David Higham Associates; Presents from my Aunts in Pakistan, from Carrying my wife, by Moniza Alvi, Bloodaxe Books, 2000; Hurricane Hits England © Grace Nichols, c/o Curtis Brown Ltd; Fantasy of an African Boy © James Berry, c/o Peters, Fraser and Dunlop; Blessing, by Imtiaz Dharker, Postcards from god, Bloodaxe Books, 1997; Sugar Cane, © Grace Nichols, c/o Curtis Brown Ltd; French Coloniel, from True Stories, © Margaret Atwood, Curtis Brown Ltd; Vultures from Beware Soul Brother, © Chinua Achebe, Reed Educational; Not My Business, © Niyi Osundare; © Bill Bryson. Extracted from A Walk in the Woods by Bill Bryson, published by Black Swan, a division of Transworld Publishers; Oh no not my baby, Department for Education and Skills; photo p.102, © Dick Makin, Getty Images (UK) Ltd; The Storm, © Theodore Roethke c/o Faber and Faber Ltd; An African Downpour, © Isaac I. Elkimimian.